# Beyond Excellence

The Art of Being, Becoming, and Serving as a Chair: Executive Coach, Mentor, and Facilitator

Severin Sorensen

V1.3

Copyright © 2023 by Severin Sorensen
All rights reserved. This book or any portion thereof
may not be duplicated or used in any manner whatsoever
without the express written permission of the publisher
except for the use of brief quotations in a book review.
Printed in the United States of America
First Printing, 2023
ISBN 9798398393934

www.aretecoach.io

# Acknowledgements

The author expresses thanks for the many current and former TEC-Vistage Chairs that have shared their stories and insights on the Arete Coach Podcast. The excerpts that appear herein were reported verbatim, with the few exceptions where editing the text made the conversation clearer. Regardless, the intent of each response remains consistent with the podcast guest's original design.

Additionally, the author is grateful to Bob Nourse's family, Ozzie Gontang, Chip Webster, and TEC Vistage Keepers of The Flame who provided numerous images for this book. All additional images including the image on the cover were prepared by Severin Sorensen using MidJourney AI with Adobe Photoshop modifications for artistic or thematic purposes.

This independently produced work acknowledges the author's past affiliation and experiences with TEC-Vistage, serving as a former TEC-Vistage Member, former Vistage Chair, and current Vistage Speaker. It includes the comments and remarks of numerous current and former Vistage Chairs on the Arete Coach Podcast. The author is grateful for TEC-Vistage support over the years of the member, chair, and speaker communities. While the body of this work speaks highly of TEC-Vistage and the Chair community, it is important to note that the author implies no endorsement of this publication by Vistage Worldwide, Inc. The errors, if any, remain those of the authors.

The terms "Vistage" and "TEC" are trademarked and copyrighted by Vistage Worldwide, Inc., and the author makes no claim of ownership over those terms.

The terms "Arete Coach Podcast" are trademarked and copyrighted by Arete Coach LLC.

# TABLE OF CONTENTS

INTRODUCTION..........................................................5
Celebrating TEC-Vistage's 65 Year Anniversary....................8
THE POWER OF VISTAGE with Conner Neill........................25
VISTAGE GROUP CULTURE with Cinder Hesterman................27
BECOMING A GREAT CHAIR with Peter Buchanan..................28
POWERFUL COACHING MOMENTS with Gail Schaper-Gordon...29
ASKING THE RIGHT QUESTIONS with Barry Goldberg............31
PURPOSE AND PASSION with Mark Fackler.......................33
GRACE NOT GRIEF with Bridget Wenman.........................35
BEING A BETTER COACH AND CHAIR with Dale Richards........36
WHAT I WISH I'D KNOWN with Mikki Williams....................37
LEVERAGING THE COMFORTABILITY SYNDROME with Cindy Hesterman.............................................................39
IMPOSTER SYNDROME with Severin Sorensen....................41
HOW WILL YOU MEASURE YOUR LIFE with Perry Maughmer...42
ACHIEVING YOUR HIGHEST POTENTIAL with Ben Griffiths.......44
HUMILITY AND LEARNING FROM MISTAKES with Steve Ramerini..............................................................45
ANTICIPATING THE WIN with Michelle Barry......................47
THREE CHALLENGES with the Late Richard Bosworth...........49
ACCOUNTABILITY WORKS with Janet Fogerty....................50
ASKING DEEPER QUESTIONS with Paul Martin...................51
STRATEGIC PLANNING with Julie Gammack......................53

ETHICS NOT FOR SALE with Mike Denning..........................54
PERSONAL PROFESSIONALS with Norma Rosenberg............55
CHANGE THE PEOPLE with Bud Carter...............................57
SHADOW OF THE LEADER with Carol Steinberg..................58
THE 'AHA' MOMENT with Jason Thompson.........................59
EMOTIONAL INTELLIGENCE with Doug Bouey......................61
A DIFFERENT RELATIONSHIP with Kathrine Crewe................62
EMPLOYEE ENGAGEMENT with Ken Stibler.........................63
LIFELONG LEARNERS with Jeanette Hobson........................65
SURROUNDING YOURSELF WITH HIGH PERFORMERS with Chip Webster....................................................................67
THE BEST VERSION OF YOURSELF with Larry Cassidy............69
THE GROUND YOU'RE STANDING ON with Tim Fulton............71
OPPORTUNITY IS NOWHERE with Tony Lewis.......................73
THE POWER OF SILENCE with Glen Warring.........................74
PASSION, PURPOSE, CALLING with Kevin McKeown...............75
WHAT'S IN YOUR WAY? with Ozzie Gontang.......................77
In Closing............................................................79
Quotes from the Vistage Chair Community.........................82
YESTERDAY & TOMORROW with Jim Handy........................84
Appendix  TEC-Vistage Chairs on the Arete Coach Podcast...136

# FORWARD

To TEC-Vistage Chairs, past, present, and future:

    This book celebrates over 65 years of Chairing. It acknowledges the contribution of the early pioneers, starting with Bob Nourse's opening words at the first "The Executive Committee" (TEC) meeting in October of 1957. After a long period of silence, Bob simply said, "Now let's get down to work." This work acknowledges Fred Chaney and Bill Hall's contribution to giving TEC legs, expanding it across the United States and around the world.

    I want to thank Severin Sorensen for his commitment to the TEC-Vistage Chair community and for his toiling to bring this book to life.

    When I joined TEC Florida in 1987, I saw it as a stepping stone to "bigger and better things". I had merged my Georgia phonebook publishing business with a bigger publishing company. If I had been a TEC member, I would have gotten better advice and stayed independent. I wanted to be in Florida for the warm weather and sailing. I was at the 30th Anniversary meeting in San Diego and briefly met Bob Nourse. I could tell it was a special group of people, but I was still recruiting and had yet to have my first meeting. All I was focused on was how to get my group rolling so I could get paid. And since I had never run a group, I had little to add to the conversations. Somewhere between year-two and three, and becoming a two CE group and Key group Chair, I began to realize that this was a calling. I can remember leaving a meeting saying to myself, "I can't believe I get paid to do this."

The glue that kept me committed was not only the connection to my members but the fast friendships I had developed in the Chair community. They were people I came to rely on for sage advice, support, and deep friendship. I had been given an opportunity to join several companies but said no. This is my life's purpose.

The life of a Chair is so rich. The Members pay to learn and get advice, but we get paid to learn, and because of all the exposure we learn more than the members. Think how many people have deep conversations with 15 or more high achievers every month? How many people are exposed to a peer community of similar wise people to further explore the wisdom of the ages? How many people get to have one-on-one dinners with five or six nationally recognized authorities on important subjects? TEC-Vistage Chairs do. The compounding of all those experiences yields a well-informed individual.

It is lonely at the top when you are running a company, and it is lonely at the end of the table when you are running a group of strong independent leaders. Only other Chairs know just how lonely it can be. At the TEC-Vistage annual Chair meetings there would be a time slot for ten plus-year Chairs to meet and talk about their experiences and share best practices. Year after year many would say we need more time together. In February 2005 as my good friend Doug Bouey and I were leaving the meeting we agreed to come up with a plan to meet that summer. We wanted to create a space where we could share our journey in life as a Chair with those who understand through our common experience. We call it *Keepers of the Flame*. Since our first gathering of 13 it has grown to as many as 100 Chairs meeting in Boulder Colorado each year. It has become an important touchstone for all who attend, exploring our life journey and meaning.

Being a Chair has blessed all of us.

Enjoy the stories in this book and think of the ripple effect each Chair has on the members, their companies, the employees and their families. We are the few who influence the few, who influence the many.

My TEC-Vistage Chairing experience inspired me to become a published poet including this poem.

## ANGELS[1]

*Trying to figure out the*
*Universe can be tiring*

*So many variables*
*So many surprises*
*So many disappointments*

*But why are we here*
*Why the hell are we here*

*To be angels for each other*
*Angels in human form*

*Angels to lift us up when we are down*
*Angels to open the door to a bigger world*
*Angels to let us know we are loved*

---

[1] From the book *Paint and Poetry, An Ekphrastic Journey* by Terry Brett & Chip Webster (2021)

May we all look forward to the next 65 years of Vistage, and our roles influencing so many powerful men and women to improve their businesses, their lives, and the lives of everyone in their prevue. It truly is a joy to be a part of such a noble work.

Signed,

Chip Webster

Chair, 1987 to 2003
TEC Florida Chair of the year 1996, 1997
Cope Award 1999
President TEC / Vistage Florida 2000 to 2013
Member, 2000 to 2013
Cofounder TEC VISTAGE
Keepers of the Flame

# INTRODUCTION

As I sit down to pen this tribute to the enduring legacy of TEC-Vistage, I am swept away in a current of memories, lessons, and profound transformations. My journey with this remarkable organization, from member to Chair, to Speaker, an appreciative beneficiary and an unofficial ambassador of the TEC-Vistage model, has shaped my understanding of leadership and growth in ways I could have never anticipated. This book, then, is more than a tribute—it is an exploration of the essence of TEC-Vistage, as seen through the unique and multifaceted role of the Chair.

In 1957, Bob Nourse laid the foundations for the TEC-Vistage model, championing a fresh approach to executive coaching and peer group facilitation. His vision was steeped in the tenets of human potential, driven by the profound belief that every executive, irrespective of their accomplishments, held the potential to ascend to greater heights through the sharing of wisdom, challenges, and experiences. This belief provided the bedrock for the role of the TEC-Vistage Chair—a role that I was deeply honored to assume from 2010 through 2018, and one that continues to guide me as I navigate my journey of service and giving back to others.

This book is an assemblage of voices, insights, and wisdom, gathered from my conversations with some of the most successful Chairs across the globe. Through my Arete Coach Podcast, a discussion-format program that explores the art and science of executive coaching, I have had the privilege of uncovering the core motivations, inspirations, techniques, and unique coaching styles that define these remarkable individuals. Their stories, captured here, present a mosaic portrait of the TEC-Vistage Chair—a role that illuminates the path towards personal and professional actualization for business leaders around the world.

The role of a Chair is akin to a conductor in an orchestra, not merely guiding the ensemble but also awakening the latent potential within each musician. Similarly, a Chair is more than an executive coach, mentor, and facilitator—they are a beacon that illuminates the path towards self-discovery and growth. As I evolved into this role, it was not only about guiding others, but it was also a journey of self-transformation.

My TEC-Vistage journey began in 1999, and the personal and professional transformations that unfolded over the years are immeasurable. Today as my daughter embarks on her own TEC-Vistage journey, like so many other multi-generational TEC-Vistage member families, the organization's impact extends to the next generation, affirming the enduring power of its model. I fully expect my other children to join TEC-Vistage groups in time.

In our competitive world, the move towards a collaborative and supportive space is not just a transition—it's a transformation. It is about 'harvesting our better angels', to borrow the evocative phrase from Lincoln, and fostering a spirit of cooperation to lift others in our world. It's about moving from a place of competition to collaboration, a transition that the TEC-Vistage Chair embodies so eloquently. I love the poetic words of Chip Webster, co-founder of the Keepers of The Flame, who in his Forward for this book shared a choice poem he wrote about angels...

> *To be angels for each other*
> *Angels in human form*
> *Angels to lift us up when we are down*
> *Angels to open the door to a bigger world.*

That is the 'call' of a Chair.

As we continue to celebrate the 65th anniversary of TEC-Vistage, I invite you to join me on this journey of exploration and celebration. This tribute is more than an acknowledgement of our shared history —it's a testament to our ongoing dedication to reach the apex of performance, embodied in the Greek term *'Arete,'* a pursuit not just of excellence, but of our highest moral virtues.

To echo the words of Abraham Maslow, we aspire to serve and to be more than ourselves. We strive for the fullest realization of our potential. This is the legacy of a TEC-Vistage Chair. This is our journey ahead.

And so, let us learn from our Chair peers whose voices echo herein on how to be good, do good, and seek to uplift others in the important role of the Chair, executive coach, mentor, and facilitator.

Signed,

Severin Sorensen

TEC-Vistage
Member (1999-2004)
Vistage Chair (2010-2018)
Vistage Speaker (2013-Present)

Host, Arete Coach Podcast
Curator, AreteCoach.io
CEO, ePraxis LLC

# Celebrating TEC-Vistage's 65 Year Anniversary

This past October, TEC-Vistage celebrated its 65th anniversary.

What a milestone!

Any company with that much history, and so many excellent people behind the scenes, has too many stories to contain in a single volume. Even so, as we celebrate that history today, we're talking to some of the people who helped build Vistage over those 65 years, who saw its transition from TEC, and inspired coaches and business leaders to create the world's foremost training and peer advisory organization.

Every successful business comes down to the people who worked to make it great. Today we look more closely at those individuals, their stories and words of wisdom, as we look forward to the next 65 years of Vistage history.

This Arete Coach Podcast episode review revisits the birth, early development, and growth of TEC, and its maturation into Vistage. This episode of the Arete Coach Podcast was recorded on January 28th, 2023, via Zoom video and also includes dozens of interview callouts from current and former Vistage Chairs and stakeholders from previous episodes recorded since April of 2020.

> *"The strength of the wolf is the pack, and the strength of the pack is the wolf"*
> – Rudyard Kipling

In pondering the power of peers and peer executive groups. My mind goes to a famous quote by Rudyard Kipling, "For the strength of the wolf is the pack, and the strength of the pack is the wolf." A wolf is made stronger by the pack, yet the strengths the individual wolf brings to the pack make the group as a whole that much stronger.

For a peer group to be effective, there must be both give and take. There is a synergy there and you want to have peer group members bringing their strengths to the group, for the strength of the wolf is the pack.

TEC-Vistage is a pack of some pretty impressive wolves, each making the whole that much stronger.

Have you ever considered that you, as a leader, are the average of the people you keep around you? If you surround yourself with "yes" men and sycophants, you risk peril to you and your kingdom. The fable of *The Emperor has no Clothes* shares the folly of such danger where even trusted advisors are afraid to tell their leader the truth for fear of reprisal. Even when the bare truth of nakedness is obvious to all onlookers, no one is willing to point it out.

The fact is, over the ages, great leaders always gather people around them who will speak the truth.

Even the brutal truth.

Anciently in Egypt and the Ottoman Empire, the Pharaohs and Sultans employed Viziers that they chose for their loyalty, temperance, wisdom, council, and keen sense of discernment. Some of these Viziers were promoted to senior leadership roles, administering great projects or overseeing key government functions. Similarly in ancient China, wise leaders sought to surround themselves with sage advisors. Consider this advice drawn from the biography of lord Shang Yang, who lived in 338 BC and was a China statesman and reformer active during the war states period, is quoted in Sima Qian's historical records stating, *"A thousand yes men cannot equal one honest advisor."*

The practice of having truth-speaking advisors and analysts around leaders continued with the privy councils of kings, queens, and monarchs. The Privy Counsellor's Oath also holds the values of confidentiality and honesty, much like today's peer groups. Consider the following excerpt for the Privy Counsellor's Oath quote:

*"You will in all things be moved, treated, and debated in counsel, faithfully and truly declare your mind and opinion, or according to your heart and conscience, and will keep secret, all matters committed and revealed unto you, or that shall be treated of secretly in counsel, so help you, God."*

Where is your privy council? Do you have a place where you meet with engaged leaders to debate, counsel, and declare opinions? Do you work with people who guide you according to their heart and conscience, giving you their best advice while providing confidentiality?

If you don't, you need to find those people. Leaders rely on their advisors.

That is why TEC-Vistage was created in the first place.

## Disclosure

Full disclosure here. I've experienced what some call the Vistage trifecta. I have been a Vistage member, a chair, and now a speaker. The observations that I share in this podcast are those of my own, or the direct quotes from other Vistage Chairs and stakeholders from years gone by. Importantly, whether assigned or informal, I would label myself as an ambassador of Vistage, as I very much value the peer group model, members, Chairs, and the core values that Vistage promotes, which are trust, caring, challenge, and growth. My own family's participation with Vistage covers 24 years of the company's 65-year history and includes my own experience as a member, Chair, and speaker. And the Vistage tradition continues with my daughter today being seated in a key executive group in Washington DC in 2022.

## The History of TEC-Vistage

In October of 2022, Vistage celebrated its 65th anniversary. Founded in 1957 by Bob Nourse, who established the company as The Executive Committee or TEC.

Bob Nourse was one of two brothers operating a family business in the 1940s and '50s in Milwaukee called Midlands. Bob was younger than his brother Claire, who was nicknamed Pinky by many. When his brother asked Bob to join the family business, Pinky had been in the company some five years already. Bob agreed, and soon thereafter Bob's brother began working as President while Bob was Vice President.

This was a time of learning for Bob. He learned that mixing family and business was tough, and he readily admitted his reservations in his autobiography. Bob writes, *"It's difficult enough working with a brother, but working for one's brother can be hell."*

Like so many other business leaders trying to build a company, balancing the human side of life with the work side of life proved challenging. But Bob always seemed to work through life's issues positively, treating them as learning opportunities instead of excuses to complain. The company operated for nearly 20 years, and over time it changed its lineup of products and services and started to sell garden tractors.

In 1954, Midlands sold several million dollars of garden tractors to Montgomery Ward, and then, to quote Bob again, *"We had the rug pulled on us."* In response to the changing market, he switched their business line to one of their competitors, and by 1957 it was evident that the company would not survive.

Closing your doors is a hard experience for any family-owned business. The end of Midlands was no different for the Nourses. Fortunately, Bob's brother was able to sell what was left of the company to pay creditors. They even ended up with a little leftover for shareholders, of which Bob was of course one.

While working for Midland, Bob had taken several business courses at the Management Institute of the University of Wisconsin. He became interested in and influenced by the fields of psychology and group dynamics, and the emerging human potential movement. He became most interested in the works of Carl Jung and Kurt Lewin. His interest in the power of seminars intensified, as did exploring how to increase human potential. He also became the President of Cambridge House, a growth center where such seminars were held.

Bob took his dividends and decided to try something different that aligned with his new interests and field of study.

## Influences on the Creation of TEC-Vistage

During the formative years immediately preceding the creation of TEC, Bob dove headfirst into the works of authors that challenged how students saw humanity in general.

The human potential movement was in full swing during this time. This cultural and intellectual undertaking obviously inspired Bob Nourse and many others to look at life and business differently. By focusing on the possibility of individuals developing their full human potential and overcoming limiting psychological and social conditions, humanity could improve in limitless ways. The movement was influenced by various fields such as psychology, philosophy, and spirituality. It was associated with the development of humanistic psychology, which emphasized self-actualization and personal growth. The human potential movement also influenced various fields such as education, therapy, and management, and it continues to have an impact on contemporary ideas about personal development, self-help, and human flourishing.

Commenting on this period, Jenny Ditzler in her 2006 article, described it as a *"period of personal transformation and personal development where it became safe to be a human being and to admit faults."*

It is this vulnerability and openness that sets the tone for greater executive peer group experiences that Bob was slowly becoming inspired to create.

Psychiatrist Carl Jung became one of Bob's first resources in creating something new in the coaching space. Jung is best known for his ideas on the human psyche, including the concept of collective unconsciousness, archetypes, and the physiological structures of the psyche. Jungs ideas of ego, the personal unconsciousness, and the self, enthralled Bob. The psychologist also developed a theory of personality types, known today as the Myers-Brigg type indicator or the MBTI. He is also known for his works on synchronicity, dream analysis, and the concept of individuation.

Another author inspiring Bob during these developmental days was Kurt Lewin, best known for his work in the field of social psychology. Lewin posited ideas about group dynamics and change management that were revolutionary. He developed the concept of action research, which emphasizes the involvement of individuals and groups in the process of identifying and solving problems in their own social systems. The Force Field Analysis Model was another of Lewin's ideas, describing the factors that drive and resist change in an organization or social system. Lewin's work also focused on the concept of unfreezing, changing, and refreezing as a model for understanding how people and groups make lasting changes forever. Additionally, his work on leadership and decision-making has a significant impact on management and organizational theory.

Abraham Maslow was another psychologist that inspired Bob. Maslow is best known for his theory of human motivation, known as Maslow's Hierarchy of Needs. The theory proposes that people have basic needs that must be met before they can focus on higher-level needs, such as self-actualization. The five levels of needs are psychological, safety, love, belonging, esteem, and self-actualization. Once these lower needs are met, people can focus on reaching their full potential or self-actualizing. Maslow's theory has had a significant impact on the field of psychology and is often used in business management and education.

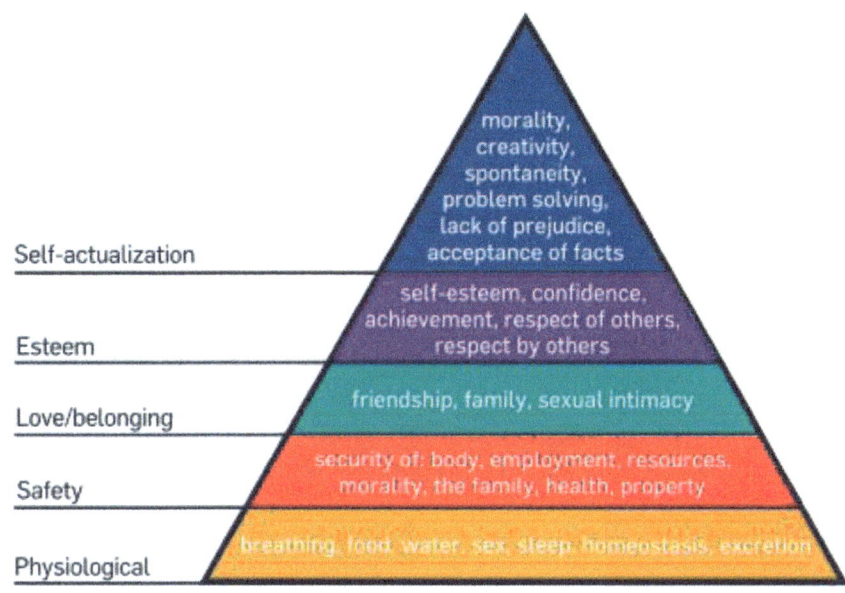

An interpretation of Maslow's hierarchy of needs, represented as a pyramid, with the more basic needs at the bottom

About this period, Dr. Vikki Brock wrote in the Source Book of History of Coaching, *"During the first years of the post-modern period that is approximately from 1950 to '65, the world saw the heightening of the Cold War, the decolonization of former European colonies, the reconstruction of Japan. We also saw the work of BF Skinner, Martin Heidegger, and Abraham Maslow begin to take currency. Their theories influenced the growth of encounter groups and the rise of the human potential movement, the proliferation of business schools, and much more."*

Maslow's ideas were influential in the human potential movement as they provided a framework for understanding how people could achieve their full potential and become the best version of themselves.

It was in this environment that Bob Nourse started what would become TEC Vistage. He wrote in his biography, *"I began exploring ways in which I might turn these avocations of mine into a vocation. I was bound and determined to retain my independence, not to go to work for another company for salary."*

In early 1957, Bob had an idea. Would 8 to 10 company presidents be interested in forming a group to solve each other's problems? He knew that many presidents paid consultants to find economic and personnel solutions. Heck, he had paid for consultants himself when he was at Midland.

The question was, would they pay to be in a group?

## The Creation of TEC (The Executive Committee)

With experience in business, corporate education, psychology, research, and a focus on group dynamics, Bob felt he was ready for the work.

The TEC experience as envisioned was a monthly peer executive group where you had access to expert resources and a monthly one-to-one coaching session. The model envisioned that a business-savvy executive would serve as coach, mentor, and facilitator of the executive peer group.

Bob plotted everything out, creating the framework for his MVP, minimally viable product, and presented the idea to several friends, his rector, a lawyer, a management consultant, an industrial psychologist, and a colleague who was a company president.

All of them encouraged him to start the group.

*Imagining Bob Nourse designing the future structure and purpose of TEC, 1957*

One of them said, "How about calling it 'The Executive Committee'?" And he replied, "Perfect!"

TEC was born.

Like Vistage Chairs today, Bob, as the first TEC Chair, started calling on business owners to join his executive peer group. He called on CEOs, generating interest in the group in the midsummer, and then in October 1957, four of his contacts showed up.

Only four.

At the end of his first meeting however, all of them said they would attend again and be willing to pay for additional meetings. Before the next summit even started, Bob had enrolled 3 more presidents into his group, and TEC was launched.

At that second meeting, Bob established group norms and procedures that were incredibly similar to how they are still done

Bob Nourse (bottom row, second from left) and the original TEC group

today. He established standards for group sizes, criteria that all members would be non-competing colleagues, that they would represent the highest-level positions within a given company (presidents or CEOs), and that they would attend full-day meetings to be held once each month.

Leaving nothing to chance, Bob even formulated how the individual meetings would be scheduled. Mornings would be spent listening to a resource specialist, something we call today a *Vistage Speaker*, to discuss a subject of group interest. In the afternoon, each member was to help solve a problem or an issue presented for discussion. A chairman would plan and conduct the individual meetings, holding monthly interviews with members to help them articulate business problems that would then be brought back to the group the following month.

Two years later, a second group was formed called TEC II, then a third group was added, and a fourth. Things began to snowball from there, and Bob Nourse invited partners to join him in the work. When Bob retired in 1980, there were thousands of TEC members from coast to coast, and in Australia and Japan as well.

## Reflections of Bob Nourse

Legendary chair Pat Murray put together some comments about Bob Nourse in April of 2006. He recalled, *"When I joined TEC, Bob was near the end of his career as a Chair. He still ran*

*TEC One and he was still available, but Jim and Harry were now leading the organization."* Pat wrote of his experience, *"We considered ourselves to be process people rather than content experts. The work, as I understood it, was focused on the depth, health, and longevity of the groups. Skill development addressed issues like listening, connecting, exploring, supporting, challenging, group dynamics, unpacking or unbundling assumptions and belief systems, and many others. All tools designed to promote deep learning."*

Pat Murray recalled a poignant recollection with Bob Nourse where he had an opportunity to sit in on one of Bob's TEC group meetings. It was an eye-opening experience. *"Bob invited me to observe, and it was quite extraordinary to see Bob's skills and the sense of rapport he had with the group. I was most struck by Bob's stillness. That is the quality that got my attention. And Bob had a lot of silence in his personality."* He continued, *"TEC is not a place where the 'new' or 'exciting' happens. You just keep going deeper."*

TEC Founder Bob Nourse

There's something to ponder there. Relationships at TEC weren't about breaking new ground, but in digging deeper to understand the partners and their problems. It was about real solutions.

Lee Thayer later wrote of Bob Nourse, *"It was not Bob's dream to create a great TEC empire. Rather, it was his dream to provide otherwise isolated CEOs with peer observation and criticism. All the while reminding them that the CEO's role was a journey, not a destination. There are a few Chairpersons and TEC members who are furthering Nourse's project as he originally saw it."*

And Bob's work has actually continued through a number of Chairs who keep the tradition alive today. They ask better questions, go deeper in discussions, and let silence do the heavy lifting.

Bob Nourse would be described in 21$^{st}$ century terms as a strong intuitive, with keen intellect, sensitivity to situations in silence, and highly developed active listing skills.

Simply put, he was a master.

Today, the organization Bob built is many times its original size with hundreds of coaching Chairs and thousands of Vistage members worldwide. As TEC grew, it employed leaders that were PhDs for Midwest business schools. These advisers were also interested in organizational psychology, structural development management, and group dynamics.

While the TEC model has been updated and refreshed, with new research underpinning training and development for Chairs, the early foundations of the model remain. And for that, I, and so many others, are grateful for the work of Bob Nourse and the coaches who helped him achieve so much. These thought leaders have continued to pioneer the executive coach-facilitated peer group model. The genius behind its success, and one of the reasons it continued strong today, is that those original core ideas work with the individuality of coaches and members.

I am personally convinced that Vistage is for every business leader…but not every business leader is right for every group. That's where Chair and group fitting and selection come into play. Everything is built around adaptability, which has allowed for pivots and shifts that helped the company thrive. Now, 65 years on, the future is in no way playing second fiddle to the past.

## Features of Vistage Peer Executive Groups Today

From the early work of Bob Nourse and his first TEC groups, all the way to the modern boardrooms of 2023, you can see many universal challenges being addressed in these peer executive groups. They are, and have always been, safe places to talk about real issues impacting the lives of the executives and their companies. They deal with family business issues, including dysfunctions and familial relationships that often impact the business and personal lives of participants. Members care about the individual and those around them. They explore the growth-edge areas of the team and their companies. They bounce ideas off other members for big opportunities, operating issues, and challenging problems using the assembly as their mastermind group. They work through confidential and often sensitive issues impacting the members in their companies. It is a regular place for openness and vulnerability.

I've had members tell me that this is the only place where they can share their most inner feelings and thoughts about what's going on in their business and lives. It is a trusted setting, an environment with ground rules to safeguard mental health, safety, and well-being. It is a place where radical candor is welcomed.

Some lovingly refer to the Vistage dynamic with the conjunctive word, "carefrontation," which means being both caring and aggressive as we address key issues that may be holding members back from reaching their full potential.

It's a place for accountability, a place where monthly members can report on their progress and be held accountable for their goals. This focus makes actions intentional and thus more likely to bring lasting change. It's a place where there's an environment that supports lifetime learning and curiosity with new resources brought to the group each month.

It's a place where bonds are built, truly creating a band of brothers and sisters able to weather any storm, together.

And outside of the monthly meetings, one-to-one executive coaching occurs where members identify key issues in their business. During these sessions, leaders are able to discuss and prepare to bring back their problems back to the group for processing with their peer executives. These problems range from supply chain issues and personnel changes, all the way to work/life balance and family strife.

Many taglines have existed for the organization over the years, but the one that seems to permeate and endure is the one that holds the most meaning to members: "Enhancing the lives of executives and their businesses," and all that entails.

That's been our mission statement for 65 years.

In 2006, TEC was rebranded into Vistage and the company has grown in intercontinental reach, members, groups, chairs, and impact. Today in 2023, Vistage is still recognized as the pioneer of executive coach-facilitated peer executive groups with thousands of members worldwide.

## Insights from Past and Present Vistage Chairs

Now, with all the background laid out, I would like to explore more deeply the unique attributes of Vistage's model. Since day-one, the primary aspect has been an executive coach or Chair facilitating a peer executive group.

Nothing more complicated than that.

And it's in its simplicity that Vistage thrives.

Our core tenets have always been judgment, discernment, active listening, wisdom, candor, and engagement. Those attributes are central to the success of our Chairs.

These are best exemplified by some of the great Vistage Chairs, past and present, and other stakeholders that represent some of Vistage's highest values.

Over the years I've spoken with many of them, always uplifted and inspired by their simple dedication to the highest principles established by Bob Nourse. Instead of having me paraphrase their thoughts, from here on out I'll let them speak for themselves.

The following excerpts are taken from my Arete Coaching Podcast where I spoke with each of these individuals and learned about their personal drive and love of coaching. I've included the episode number for each to facilitate any further listening and a deeper dive into their processes and brilliance. You can find a list of current and former TEC-Vistage Chairs who have been interviewed from April 2020 through June 2023 in the appendix of this book.

Now sit back, read, ponder, and enjoy the words of giants among us in the Chair community.

Keepers of the Flame 2022

# THE POWER OF VISTAGE

## Episode #1037 with

## Connor Neill, Vistage Spain

**Conor Neill:** You know, Vistage might appear to be a business organization, but as the trust builds in a Vistage group, you start to realize there's a very blurry line between what is business and what is personal.

What's important to a human being starts to be the focus of the group work.

Vistage is, at the beginning, certainly a lot more goal-oriented. In Vistage, we are interested in what your aspirations are as a business; where do you want to be in three to five years, and what changes are you willing to put around you and work on inside yourself to achieve those growth goals over the coming years? So certainly, at the beginning, the conversation with a Vistage potential member is about, 'What are your growth goals that you don't know how you're going to achieve from where you are right now?' If you've got an aspiration, if you've got a dream, but you don't have the plan, now I'm interested in speaking to you.

With Vistage, there is an individual, the group Chair, who is deeply interested in creating a culture in the group of sharing with vulnerability, of clarity, and honesty about what we really want in life. And having that position of being able to call people out when they say, "I think you're coasting. I think you're backing away from the level that we're able to go to," is important. In an EO forum, no one has the right to call you out and say, "That's not enough."

I'm a peer.

In Vistage, there is a person who is there almost precisely to call out anyone who's coasting, who's giving, who's phoning it in.

So much of the work we do at Vistage is in the group dynamics. As a Chair, how do you raise up the level of honesty, the level of trust, between the members of the group, the level of depth that we go to in processing the challenges that each are facing, and the level of accountability that if you make a promise, having used the group's time, someone's going to keep track of it?

In Vistage, there's a greater interest in seeing your life moving forward, seeing you making measurable, deliberate progress in the quality of the relationships around you, in the quality of the financial decisions you're taking, in the quality of the strategy such that your business three years from today is ready for a crisis.

I guess the real power of Vistage is, I think Tom Landry says, *"A coach is somebody who tells you what you don't want to hear, shows you what you don't want to see, so that you can be the person you've always known that you could be."* A Chair is not a master in asking great questions. A Chair is a master in helping others ask the great questions. In a recent Vistage training, someone said, "The most important conversation in any relationship is the conversation that we're not having."

# VISTAGE GROUP CULTURE

## Episode #1051 with
## Cindy Hesterman, Vistage Florida.

**Severin Sorensen:** So, what was the culture of the group that you intentionally sought to put together?

**Cindy Hesterman:** I actually created a vision of a world-class group, and I shared that at my very first group meeting. So, once I got my 8 together, I think I had nine actually at my first meeting. We went through that, and I shared my vision, and I made sure that they were in alignment with that vision. We created what we wanted to become, knowing it might take us some time to get there.

And it was everyone contributing, everyone being open to feedback, everyone leaving their ego at the door, and coming in to learn from one another. And then, of course, a full group. And so those were the things that we strive to achieve. Very diverse people, backgrounds, experiences, and that kind of thing.

# BECOMING A GREAT CHAIR

## Episode #1067 with
## Peter Buchanan, TEC Canada

**Severin Sorensen:** When new chairs come into your academy, what is the greatest myth or perception that they have to overcome to become a great chair?

**Peter Buchanan:** Well, even though we talk to them about it when we're recruiting them, they come in thinking that it's really their experience in business, their expertise, that is going to make the difference. They get into telling people what to do. "You need to do this; you need to do that." And one of the things I've always emphasized is, people don't care how much you know until they know how much you care.

So really, it's about establishing a relationship with a prospective member. That's job one. You've got to build that relationship. They have to trust you. And once they trust you, then you can have the deep conversations, then you can dig in with them and go to those places that maybe they don't want to talk about, or maybe they've never talked about with anybody. But if you have trust, you can help take them there. And that creates, for me, that creates just a really strong connection with a member. And they tend to stay for a long time because they know, as I said, it's the only place in the world where they can have a conversation.

# POWERFUL COACHING MOMENTS

## Episode #1053 with

## Gail Schaper-Gordon, Ph.D. from Vistage California

**Severin Sorensen:** Can you remember your best day ever as a coach?

**Gail Schaper-Gordon:** Oh, gosh. I had one recently. It was so phenomenal: a group meeting where I knew that I had someone who had a really important way to express something. He had an insight that he had gained as a result of our one-to-one and it related to someone who had an issue to process and that I felt was going to contribute to everyone in the meeting.

People were watching, they said, "We were watching you; we did not know where you were going."

And I said, "I didn't know either, but I knew where I wanted to get."

Someone had written a rap and it was a story. Part of the words are, "I was never meant to live. I was never meant to live" because he was born dead as a child. And he is this amazing athlete, human being, who is just so talented and creative.

That touched everybody and took everybody down to an emotional level.

Then I processed an issue with someone, and he was kind of stuck. I was at a place where, this is how you process issues, and you got to do this, this, and this. I just said, "Okay, I'm not gonna do what we're gonna do because now... everybody else, I know you're all in a place." I had them do an exercise to talk about their own ways and what are the things from their past that get in their way when they are facing really challenging moments.

And so, everyone in the room went through this transformative, emotional experience, at the same time. It was just, it was like being... just moving people along to where they were. That feeling in that place and that moment was just magical. And to share that moment with all of them and then how they shared that experience with each other was just...

**Severin Sorensen:** That's a great meeting when that happens. I remember years ago, it's been over 10 years when I was in Chair training Pat Hyndman said, "Just be grateful for the first time a crisis hits your group because if you'll lean into it and go into it, it will bond them, and they will understand what's important for them."

**Gail Schaper-Gordon:** Yeah, absolutely.

# ASKING THE RIGHT QUESTIONS

## Episode #1011

### Barry Goldberg, Vistage Arkansas

**Severin Sorensen:** As an executive coach, oftentimes we're seeking to ask powerful questions. What are some powerful questions that you may have asked clients in the past and perhaps an outcome or two?

**Barry Goldberg:** Well, of course, you hope every question is a powerful question, but they're not. I was with a guy who is a senior vice president of a large manufacturer agonizing over a decision. Because it was gonna impact people's lives. He'd been agonizing for a week and a half, and all the data he was ever gonna have was there, and he was agonizing about making a decision.

Finally, I said, "Look, fast forward 30 years from now. What's the story that you want your daughter, that one there in the picture, to be telling her kids? Not about the decision, but about who you were and the way you made that decision?"

Well, he did not thank me for the question. He said, "That's not fair." I said, "My job's not to be fair." And once we got through another cycle, he got to what was important to him. That led him to what his strategy was gonna be going forward.

I have this thing that I believe that everything we need in a coaching conversation shows up in the first 2 minutes; 2 to 5 minutes. You're walking in and, "Hey, how you doing?" and, "Nice seeing you! Got your coffee?" and all that and, "What's going on?" Amongst that, he said, "Oh yeah, I'm a grandfather now." "Great!" I had no idea that was gonna be useful. But somehow in those first moments, either some data or the pattern of what you're gonna be talking about is gonna be reflected in the way the conversation happened. But if I can be present for that 2 minutes, then I have weaponry going forward.

The other one that comes up is not really a question. So, I had 5 minutes to walk around the hall with this woman and get to know her, and then we were gonna sit down and do an observed coaching. And she got into this thing about "I got this employee, and I just can't make her do what she's gotta do, and I don't know what to do. I don't know what the problem is, and I just don't... I can't figure it out." And there was no moving her. "You've been asking about 'why' for 15 minutes. The question is, what do you want to do about it? What do you want to do? Let's start with what you want to do." "Well, I don't know why she..." "I don't care why she, and I don't care why you. Tell me what you would like to do."

And then sometimes the very best question is none at all. I got one guy who I still coach. He and I go off-and-on for about 6 months every 2 years, and we go walk around his office. If he simply wants to talk about something confidential, we would walk into a copy room or something. I just get out of the way and let him go, right? No question is the best question in that case. "I'm hearing this. What do you think about that?" "Hmm? Did I get this?" If he wants to pay me to do that, because no one else will, I'm happy to be his sounding board.

# PURPOSE AND PASSION

## Episode #1129

### Mark Fackler, Vistage Chair

**Severin Sorensen:** Before his passing, Clayton Christensen wrote a powerful book, *How Will You Measure Your Life?* How will you measure your life?

**Mark Fackler:** Part of me says measuring is too objective, but I understand the sentiment behind it. I will measure my life by the people who say, "Thank you," but just as important are the people who don't. I will measure by my life, by the impact, the positive impact that I can make in this world.

**Severin Sorensen:** Tell me the mindset of the person that is most suited to becoming a Chair.

**Mark Fackler:** Wow. I love that! I'm always trying to recruit Chairs. I just said this to someone a few days ago, "You should become a Chair." He's a 45-year-old, not quite a C-suite executive VP. And it was curiosity, it was humbleness. It was a ton of experience.

I think experience is very important.

You have to have stories and he had a lot of stories. But I think I asked the question right after I saw his curiosity and we were in a Vistage meeting. He's an alumni from my MBA group and I have three alumni who get to sit in the groups. And his questions are always so spot-on without judgment, without blame. Just a thoughtful question and a "tell me more" attitude. I think that's what makes a great Chair.

# GRACE NOT GRIEF

## Episode #1120

### Bridget Wenman, Vistage Chair

**Severin Sorensen:** Do you have a personal mantra that guides you today?

**Bridget Wenman:** Anybody that knows me over the last few years, I've developed one that I use a lot.

And that is grace, not grief. Man, there's enough grief in the world, I don't need to be adding to it.

I always think about that.

If I'm irritated about something or if I feel like I should stand up and say something, I just am really careful. And I heard something the other day; I was watching something about the Royal family, and they used this question, they said, "Does it need to be said? Does it need to be said by me? And does it need to be said in this moment?" And I loved that. I will always remember that.

I try to think, "Am I really adding value?" And so, to me, that's part of the grace, not grief. If it doesn't bring light or happiness or health or anything of value to someone else, I'm really going to try not to give them any more grief than they already have.

# BEING A BETTER COACH AND CHAIR

## Episode #1124

### Dale Richards, Former Vistage Chair

**Severin Sorensen:** What have you learned about being an executive that has helped you be a better coach?

**Dale Richards:** One of the topics that I talk about is my productivity pyramid, which is trademarked and its goals, coaching, accountability, and rewards, and including in that is active listening, which is we were created with two ears and one mouth. But we tend to be active talkers instead of active listeners. And I think executives need to understand, first of all, people need goals. They need mentoring. When they have goals and they're mentored as a coach monthly, and they use the techniques of active listening, asking questions, helping them to be engaged, you're going to increase your productivity. So, I believe that one of the key things really is goals, coaching, accountability, rewards, and being an active listener. Those are the key metrics of an executive to be successful.

# WHAT I WISH I'D KNOWN

## Episode #1010

### Mikki Williams, Vistage Chicago

**Severin Sorensen:** So, looking back at your journey as a coach, what is a lesson you learned recently that you wish you'd have learned many years ago?

**Mikki Williams:** I don't know how recently it is, but if anybody listening knows about DISC personality styles or any of the assessments that are out there, I am your classic, High D Secondary I, which means I'm a bottom line, get to the point, horrible listener. My personality loves to talk, horrible listening. I think what came for me is even though I'm a DISC trainer, you know, 'physician heal thyself,' was OK, you have the natural tendency to be a terrible listener, own that, which means I have to work harder. I have to have a certain awareness when I'm coaching that you can't just lapse into, "Well, this is who I am." Part of me wants to be the best coach I am, which makes me exhausted, more so at the end of the day than an average person who has a natural tendency for. So, for me, that was the biggest "ah-hah!" Using what I knew from assessments, various assessments, that this is not my gift and I have to work at it. And so, I do. I watch people like you who nod actively or who pick up your last word. I listen for that, so I become a better coach. But that was something I didn't realize in the beginning. I didn't own that natural tendency, I just showed up.

**Severin Sorensen:** Listening and appearing to be listening are vital as we learn to actively listen better.

So, what is your "why?" Do you have a "why" that gives you purpose or drive, that gives you energy?

**Mikki Williams:** Yeah. You know, my "why" was discovered in reflection and it makes so much sense to me. My "why" is legacy. That's always been what drives me. The fact that I've been on this earth, that I've left a mark, or impacted people's lives in some way. And I think that's something I didn't always know, but it became clearer through each profession that I went to and really came to fruition. As a coach.

# LEVERAGING THE COMFORTABILITY SYNDROME

## Episode #1051 with

## Cindy Hesterman, Vistage Florida.

**Severin Sorensen**: What were your secrets of success when you finally got that first group launched?

**Cindy Hesterman**: Well, I think the biggest thing was I had a bit of imposter syndrome. Especially after that fiasco we had, as far as a marketing event. And I realized, "Wow, maybe I'm not cut out for this, after all. Maybe Richard and Bill back all those years ago didn't see something in me or didn't see the right things in me."

So, I hired a coach, and I had that coach help me with my mindset and shifting my mindset and realize, you know what, those might not have been the right people for me, and I'm going to go find the right people. And if I'm passionate about what I do and what I believe Vistage can do, which clearly, I am, then those people will be arriving and showing up and I will be able to select them for my groups. And that's exactly what happened.

So it was that mindset shift that I had from that coaching experience. She was a great coach. She taught me a lot about where I was on the emotional scale, which wasn't very, very positive or very high up and helped me get higher and higher through a practice of gratitude and all the other things that great coaches can do when asking the right questions.

# IMPOSTER SYNDROME

## Episode #1130
## Severin Sorensen, Former Vistage Chair

**Severin Sorensen:** I go back to the pop psychologist Adam Grant there at Wharton, and in one of his books he talked about the value of imposter syndrome. Because of that 'uncomfortability' in those first few years where when you're doing it, you are doing your best job and all of that, it's only when you get through the year, you're like, oh, wow, I could have done that better. Here's what I've learned. And so, we're learning, and it's that edge of the, because we want to do great work because we want to do least harm because we want to help people.

We lean in, we grow, we take certification courses, we apply new methods, we bring meditation, we bring other things to it so that the entire experience, the theater of the room, that group becomes something powerful for the people there. And so, I definitely think that, when people say imposter syndrome, I really don't like the label imposter and it might be better called the 'Uncomfortability Syndrome.'

And because of my "uncomfort," my discomfort, I'm going to use that edge to lean in it, into it to do something truly great.

# HOW WILL YOU MEASURE YOUR LIFE

## Episode #1130

### Perry Maughmer, Vistage Chair

**Severin Sorensen:** Clayton Christensen also wrote a powerful book. It was called, how *Will You Measure Your Life?* How are you going to measure your life?

**Perry Maughmer:** I don't have to. It's going to be up to somebody else after I'm gone.

What I want to focus on is just doing right by the people in front of me and I, and again, I go back to Wesley's quote. I'm just going to do all the good I can, as long as I can, for as many people as I can, as frequently as I can, and whatever measurement that turns out to be, that'll be all right by me.

**Severin Sorensen:** You're a deep thinker. So, I'm going to ask you a question. I don't always ask people, if you could solve one human problem, what would it be?

**Perry Maughmer:** Without a doubt, it would be to wake people up to the fact that they always have a choice, even when it's not the choice they would prefer. Because I think people lose sight of the fact that they're, they are in control of their lives. They have a choice. They can make a different choice. It isn't always easy, it isn't always fun, but they, I think I see too many people just sit back and say what else was I going to do? You had a choice, and you can choose again tomorrow.

# ACHIEVING YOUR HIGHEST POTENTIAL

## Episode #1091

### Ben Griffiths, Former Vistage Chair

**Ben Griffiths**: I've said many times coming to this work was life, the universe, teaching me that I don't really own or control anything in life. And it was clearly a lesson I needed to learn because that was the lesson in front of me at the time.

I'm here to live a mantra that I call CCIR, be current, connected, involved and relevant. If you're going to have impact as a coach, you can't have that impact by telling people what to do.

You have that impact by leading them through an exploration themselves. It's more about the questions than the answers.

This is where Arete comes in. Arete in ancient Greek is about the pursuit of excellence and achieving your highest potential. That's really what it boils down to pursuit of excellence, achieving your highest potential. It is about supporting the people who choose to come on this part of the journey with us in pursuing excellence and achieving their highest potential.

# HUMILITY AND LEARNING FROM MISTAKES

## Episode #1007

### Steve Ramerini, Former Vistage Chair

**Steve Ramerini:** The best lesson, though, I think I probably ever learned was that successful people become successful because they've made a lot of mistakes. And I always thought, I'm an idiot. I make all these mistakes. But if you make mistakes, you can learn anything and you can improve and you can find a better way. That was a very important lesson. Even successful people, probably the more successful you are, the more mistakes you've made because you kept on trying and trying and you ultimately kept on improving to become more successful and achieve your goals.

So, I think one of the most powerful questions you can ask anyone is 'How can I help you?' How can I be of assistance? What is it that you need? And questions along the line that demonstrate that you're interested, you truly care about them, and that you're not just there to hear sounds. So that's probably, I think, the most powerful question. Another question is, "Have you thought this through?" and "Tell me how you thought this through." So, this way, I get an insight as to, what were the pressures, what were the influences, on how they arrived at this point.

I think those are probably the two most powerful questions I could ask.

# ANTICIPATING THE WIN

## Episode #1094

## Michelle Barry, Vistage Massachusetts

**Severin Sorensen:** Wayne Gretzky has this quote, and I want you to explain the quote for our listeners. His quote is basically that in hockey, *"You don't skate to where the puck is, you skate to where it's going to be."* Tell us about that and how that applies to business.

**Michele Barry:** I think everything is about anticipation, right? Everything's moving all the time. So, if you think about hockey, hockey's a very fast-moving game, right? People are moving. All the players are moving all the time and there is nothing that is where it is. Because where it is, when you're holding the puck on your stick and you're looking at where somebody is, by the time the puck gets to where they are, it's where they *were* and no longer where they *are*, right? So, you have to pass to where they're going. If you're receiving a pass, you have to be moving in a direction that makes sense for your team and for the play so that you're all in sync with the constant motion. And to me, that's just a metaphor for life really. At what point does the world just stop? At some point, don't we all just wish everything would just stop and we could catch up, and just call a timeout and just catch up on all the things that are piling up? But that's not how it goes. Businesses are constantly moving. The world around us is constantly changing. And we cannot, as leaders and as executive coaches of leaders, we cannot help anybody if we're prepared for today. We have to be constantly anticipating tomorrow and preparing for tomorrow and leading our organizations into tomorrow. We help to create tomorrow. We help to define tomorrow, but today is just the launching point to getting to tomorrow.

# THREE CHALLENGES

## Episode #1001

### The Late Richard Bosworth, TEC-Vistage Chair, UK

**Richard Bosworth:** Roselinde Torres summed up the challenge for all of us as coaches, facilitators, and ideation people. There are three challenges for the 21st-century leader:

1. How do you broaden your sources of information and ideas?
2. How do you extend and diversify your network?
3. How willing are you to let go of the past and step out into the unknown?

Those are 3 questions that have come to mean so much to me. I am driven by helping people to see things through fresh eyes and look at different ways of doing things. I want to inspire them to do that. That's also the critical part about it. Bringing together a diverse group of business leaders and engaging them in thought-provoking conversations that lead them to take decisively different action. That's the point. It's not about just having the conversation and saying, "That was nice." It's thought-provoking conversations with often ideas planted in there that they haven't thought about.

# ACCOUNTABILITY WORKS

## Episode #1036

### Janet Fogerty, Vistage Colorado

**Severin Sorensen:** Tell me about your member experience. Not everybody has actually been a Vistage member, and there are many people who are probably wondering about peer groups and so on. What was it like to be a member and then how was it different being a chair?

**Janet Fogarty:** Well, in a way it was like having 15 coaches all at once on a hot seat. But I usually say that when I finally accepted, I can look up and out and outside of my business and get into a peer group, they had a 2x4' with my name on it. It's like, oh my god, I wish I would've gotten there 15 years earlier.

So, when I talk about the hard questions that I leaned into, those were where I got some of the hard questions and I thought, "How dare they? I'm at the top of my game" and all of that. To this day they were gut punchers and made me stop and made me rethink. I had never designed my life. So, by them asking me, "What do you want? Why are you doing that? Why do you have so many offices?" Because I had just gone with the flow and been absorbed into things and grew that way and had never put my own path ahead of me, I wasn't watching for what was coming. I was agile and I craved new ideas. That's why I was loving being in a TEC group.

# ASKING DEEPER QUESTIONS

## Episode #1059

## Paul Martin, TEC Canada

**Severin Sorensen:** Questions are one of the tools of coaches. What are some of your go-to questions or powerful questions you've asked?

**Paul Martin:** Questions are the tools of coaches. Going back to my journalism world, questions are the tool of a journalist too. It's the interview process. So, for me, it is always about that.

In journalism they will teach you this question, "And how did that make you feel?" And you watch it on TV, it drives me bonkers. This is one I think is better... I would go like this: "Now you just said that. Why? It obviously has got some share of mind because it came out of your mouth. Why is that important? Why should I be even listening or why did that become the thing that you said? What's so important about that?"

So, I always ask, "Why is that important? What is the thought process you have?" And it's amazing what exploration you can have that comes from that question. I just challenge them to always say, "Is that the only measure that's out there?" Or dig deeper, right? That's that whole notion; conventional wisdom, but what are we really saying here? And can you play devil's advocate? I think that's one of the beautiful roles that you can play as a coach is to always challenge conventional wisdom and say, "Yeah, you've always thought like that, but so what?"

Keepers of the Flame 2006

# STRATEGIC PLANNING

## Episode #1088
### Julie Gammack, Vistage Iowa

**Julie Gammack:** If somebody asks us a question, it causes us to think of different alternatives and not be dug into being right. I'll never forget, I had a member one time who was taking phone calls. He'd get up and pick up a phone call. He was just on the brink of closing this one deal. He'd come back and he'd say, "They want too much…" And one of the people in the group said, "How does this acquisition fit your strategic plan you shared with us a couple of months ago?" It was like, deer in the headlights; it didn't fit the strategic vision at all. It was the art of the chase, the art of the deal he just wanted.

**Severin Sorensen:** It was about winning.

**Julie Gammack:** It was about winning. It was about winning. He just had one question. He went to the phone, and he canceled the deal. And of course, now they're, 'Oh my god!' The sellers were, 'Oh no, come back. We'll give you this. We'll give you that. We'll give you that.' No, it doesn't fit into our plan. But that was a fascinating example of the power of a question.

# ETHICS NOT FOR SALE

## Episode #1093

## Mike Denning, Vistage Arizona

**Severin Sorensen:** Do you have any examples where the group has shown great power?

**Mike Denning:** Oh yeah. Dozens of examples. My favorite one of those kinds of stories has to do with a member who was presenting an issue to a group and was talking about the fact that he had a salesperson, account manager, whatever, who had this relationship with this potential client that had, for sake of argument, let's just call it this 'Million-Dollar' contract on the table. He was concerned that this salesperson was toxic from a culture point of view within the organization. This member was so concerned about closing this deal before he took action with the employee that he was willing to put up with the damage that was being done within his company, because of this person, in order to get the money off the table.

The group, this one guy, and of all people, it was a commercial banker in the group that just tore him apart. The banker said, "Let me get this straight. So, your ethics are for sale?" I will never forget that line as long as I live.

# PERSONAL PROFESSIONALS

## Episode #1005

## Norma Rosenberg, Vistage New York

**Norma Rosenberg:** This is a real conversation that took place, about 15 years ago and it taught all of us a lot.

I had a guy that was running a public relations company with a little bit of association management, trade associations, all kinds of associations. The company he was running was in New York and he had the opportunity to buy a company in Atlanta that was much bigger than his and would have quadrupled the size of his overall business. So, he brought this to the table, and I always have some financial geniuses in the group that I run because I'm not a financial genius and we need that. The men in the room always pounce on the finances, and they start projecting the numbers 3, 5, years from now. Somebody in that room jumped up to the whiteboard and did a whole lot of numbers, and I let that go on for about 45 minutes.

Meanwhile, I had in that group, Ruth Abram, who was the founder of the Tenement Museum in Manhattan, and she was very quiet. She had a black binder, and she was taking notes and she said nothing for that 45 minutes. And then when there was a little silence in the room, "You told us two weeks ago that your personal goal is to spend more time traveling with your wife, coach your son's soccer team, and get closer to your teenage son. How is it that going to

Atlanta 3 days a week to run this business that you're going to acquire and grow the company, how is that going to jive with your personal goals?"

There was this dead silence in the room and everybody's thinking, "Why didn't I think of that?"

Ruth thought of that.

She's from the not-for-profit. So, I always have a mix of people who are, first of all, human beings and secondly in the business world. You have people that can put it all together when you have a group of different people. Ruth was the one that got Peter to think about getting his number 2 person to go to Atlanta 3 days a week so that he could keep his marriage and his family life intact and get closer to his kids. And now 35, 40 years later, the teenage son, he's running the Washington office. The marriage stayed intact, so it all worked out because Ruth sat there and got him to think about his personal goals together with his business goals. Works like that.

# CHANGE THE PEOPLE

## Episode #1016

## Bud Carter, Vistage Georgia

**Bud Carter:** Over the course of time, like you, I've met a lot of young coaches, and sometimes...maybe it's just ego or maybe it's naivety, they just try to answer and solve the client's problems.

I don't think that is the highest and best calling.

I think asking questions that cause people to think differently is. And sometimes they solve their own problems just when you get them talking about it. They have to verbalize it in order to solve the issue. But it's my ability to ask questions because, goodness knows, I don't have a lot of answers.

**Severin Sorensen:** I want to talk about pithy quotes. Give me a quote that you have used that has caused somebody to move from their position or to think a new thought they hadn't thought before.

**Bud Carter:** From Michael Cammack. He said, *"If you can't change the people, change the people."* And I had a member who was bemoaning this one employee, "So unproductive and I just can't get him aboard to do this, that, and the other." And you know, I said, "You got the book? Look in the index. Look under Michael Cammack and find a quote, *"If you can't change the people, change the people"* It is so true, so true.

# SHADOW OF THE LEADER

## Episode #1031

## Carol Steinberg, Vistage Pennsylvania

**Carol Steinberg:** I am constantly using quotes. In fact, I do a handout at every meeting, and on the cover of the handout there is always a leader, doesn't always have to be a business leader, but a leader and a quote.

From my experiences in being in high-potential executive development courses, there are two things that I constantly quote, and I constantly remember. One is *'Shadow of a Leader.'* What kind of a shadow are you casting?

I'm constantly reminding people that whether they're the executive or the emerging leader just coming up the ladder, or they're a parent or whatever role, what shadow are you casting? People look up to you. You don't have to have a title of leader or whatever. You can be an individual contributor and you're still a leader. What is that shadow you're casting that people are looking at and either saying, "I want to be like that person", or "I never want to appear like that person." So, I'm really into the shadow of the leader. Also, something that has stayed with me and that I remember is, assume innocence. And I can't tell you how valuable that one has been for me.

# THE 'AHA' MOMENT

## Episode #1071

### Jason Thompson, Vistage Utah

**Jason Thompson:** What I powerfully came to understand was an "aha!"

What's an 'aha' moment you had as you've started to dive into the neuroscience side of what you called neuro-plasticity for business? Taking it back to the individual.

You've always heard about the gut; you take your gut feeling. Well, there's actually science that can stand behind the fact that there's many different aspects that go into us as we're sizing up or internalizing more than just reading the room. It's like feeling the room in addition to looking at how people are sitting. How are they talking? Just those subtle differences and really honing those things in.

That's why I used the word "art." I like how you used the word "dance". It's very subtle. There's a lot that goes into it. But I think as we come to better understand that those subtle 1% changes, if you will, multiplied with our group, and how we can become better. That way will have profound impacts on how we make decisions for our organization. So yeah, it's very powerful and it is a dance.

**Severin Sorensen:** It is so interesting! Early coaches struggle with what is the right question? Middle-life coaches, if you will, struggle with how do I truly listen to that? And the advanced or mastery coaches dance in the moment with no objective, other than to help them create their best self, their best solution, realizing that those emotions can be leveraged.

It's all energy.

But if you can shift the energy to the things most important, that is wonderful. When the question is asked in such a way, and silence is brought to bear, that they can take ownership for their emotion, they can anchor a great launch, if you will, like a track star anchoring at the little blocks as they're getting out.

And it's exciting.

Keepers of the Flame 2007

# EMOTIONAL INTELLIGENCE

## Episode #1079

## Doug Bouey, TEC Canada

**Doug Bouey:** I wish that everybody had greater emotional intelligence. It would help a lot.

A lot of people just don't.

When the pressure is on, they operate out of visceral response and that visceral response often gets them in a lot of trouble. They are impulsive. They speak off-the-cuff without any consideration, and they say things that can't be unsaid, or they do things that can't be undone. Now, the thing is that I think many people say, "Those can't be fixed." And that was so often the starting point that we would be met with is, "Oh you can't do anything about that." But the truth is no, you *can*. In fact, people grow enormously by practicing fixing fractures. They discover in themselves that they are really bigger than the person that they thought they were. And they can learn that emotional intelligence by simply attacking and resolving a difference between people. It's really empowering for people.

**Severin Sorensen:** I think of that, and I'm reminded of this poem. "*This is the grave of Michael Day. Who died maintaining his right of way. He was right. Dead right, as he sped along. But he's just as dead as if he'd been wrong.*"

# A DIFFERENT RELATIONSHIP

## Episode #1015

### Kathrine Crewe, TEC Canada

**Severin Sorensen:** What is the role of a Chair or a coach?

**Katherine Crewe:** I think everybody else in their lives probably backs down. I mean, they own the company or they're the CEO. And even if in their heart they might want to push back or say "no," or whatever, they don't, purely based on the authority relationship.

The relationship with the Chair is supposed to be different than that.

The group is supposed to be different than that.

The group is supposed to catch you on your blind side and warn you that you're off. I've seen that happen and I've seen the power in that. I just felt that, and that's part of TEC. To me, that's really the richness of the peer group. You're in a place where there is no judgment, but you're among peers and no one's going to let you fall off the cliff either.

# EMPLOYEE ENGAGEMENT

## Episode #1075

## Ken Stibler, Vistage Texas

**Severin Sorensen:** What is the value you think that your groups receive from you? What does that kind of 'theater of the room' put together like?

**Ken Stibler:** Really good question. That's changed over time.

When I first started in Vistage I thought, "Hell, everybody wants me because I'm the great mind in the room," and it was my job to answer every one of the questions. And the shift really, and it's the quote, right: *"It's not my job to answer the questions. It's my job to question the answers."*

I've gotten more courageous. I have no problem putting a mirror up to other people. I have courage there. But I'm also a tactician and, I'm one of these where you've got to make sure that there's clarity in the room. That your employees, and I speak on employee engagement, and I've got 28 clients and members that have one Top 100. In order to do that, engagement is a huge side of that.

So, we really work on the employee engagement side of it. But it's really clarity in the message and I make sure that people are real with themselves. My group cries, we laugh, we share, a lot of old-time members as you would suspect. But we get after it, I think in my group right now, I've got 20 CEOs and I think 12 of them are 'Top 100 Best Places to Work' companies. So that's not one of those days I can just dial in

**Severin Sorensen:** You gotta be present.

**Ken Stibler:** Yeah, you gotta show up for that thing, right? Half women, and half men. I'm honored that they entrust me to work with them, and challenge them, and help them grow. They help me grow as much as I help them grow, I think.

# LIFELONG LEARNERS

## Episode #1030

### Jeanette Hobson, Vistage New York

**Severin Sorensen:** Tell us about your selection process for a new person that you're going to coach. What are your screening criteria?

**Jeanette Hobson:** The criteria that I use relates to Number 1: is this person a lifelong learner? And you can tell if they are when you find out what they're interested in and how they spend their time. That's a real important one for me. How does the person embrace the idea that they're going to be told things that they don't want to hear? Because the whole purpose of coming into a peer group is to hear things that you may not want to hear.

If that's not what you want, then don't come into a peer group.

So, in my conversations with people, I will purposely, through the questions that I ask them, plant things that are maybe a little bit different than what it would appear their direction is. And I want to see how curious they are about that. Do they just dismiss it out of hand or are they willing to talk about it a little bit and play with it a little bit? If so, it would indicate that they're open, they're willing to hear something different.

You know, people talk about vulnerability and that is certainly important. However, nobody's going to be vulnerable until they trust. So, you almost have to get the person in the room to see if the environment exudes enough trust and that person is willing to be part of that environment that's trusting.

# SURROUNDING YOURSELF WITH HIGH PERFORMERS

## Episode #1092

### Chip Webster, Vistage Florida

**Severin Sorensen:** As a lifetime learner, what did you do to take your level of performance from where you were to where you could even serve at an even higher level?

**Chip Webster:** I'm an experiential learner, right? Some people can sit down and read a book and walk away and be a better person. I sit down and read a book and I'm stimulated and get some interesting things. But being around really good high performers is where I learned.

I spent as much time as I could with the Richard Carr's and the Larry King's and the Fred Chaney's of the world. There's a whole long list I can give you of COPE winners that have become fast friends. I wouldn't be who I am today if it wasn't for my association with these people. Ozzie started Chair Net and there was a great exchange there, but I could pick up the phone and call Ozzie, or I could pick up the phone and call Rick Martin or, pick a name and say, "What did you do? How did you do this? What do you think about this? Here's my situation…"

I believe we become the average of the 10 people we hang out with. Between my members who are really high performing, and the Chairs who are really high performing, somehow, I managed to raise a little bit up.

**Severin Sorensen:** yeah.

**Chip Webster:** Towards the top.

**Severin Sorensen:** You definitely need to have a pack. Rudyard Kipling said, *"The strength of the wolf is the pack."* And when you surround yourself with great people, as you just mentioned Richard Carr, Larry King, Fred Chaney, that was wonderful. I love the community and the richness to have conversations like we're having right now, with people who have learned, sacrificed, shared the journey.

**Chip Webster:** I am the luckiest man in the world.

**Severin Sorensen:** You are pretty lucky. But you know what, preparation favors luck, doesn't it?

**Chip Webster:** It sure does.

Keepers of the Flame 2009

# THE BEST VERSION OF YOURSELF

## Episode #1009

## Larry Cassidy, Vistage California

**Severin Sorensen:** What's your 'why?'

**Larry Cassidy:** Many years ago, a member of mine, we spent 25 years together and I still sit in on the board of one of his companies a couple times a year, gave me a book. And in the book, he said that he believed that his mission in life was to become the best possible version of himself. And that along with Covey's, "Begin with the end in mind," will be the second most impactful thing that really kind of whacked me.

That changed my focus as a Vistage Chair, and as a coach, and as a person.

Not that I look back and say that I wasn't trying to do that, but I wasn't intentional about it. And that's my 'why' today. I tell the people I work with "You come into Vistage, or you hire me, because you think you want to run your business better…and you do, and we'll work on that.

And you will.

Vistage members tend to do, frankly, far better than the average member out there in terms of performance. But the real reason you should be in a group like this, and the real reason we should work together is that you want to become the best version of yourself. Because if you can pull that off, the impact on everybody in your life is profound. But you've got to work, you've got to work hard at it, and you've got to be willing to put it out there with a bark on. You can't be just smoothing everything off. You've got to be willing to play if you're going to become a better version of yourself.

I'm a believer that people do what they need to do when the pain of doing it becomes less than the pain of not doing it. And the group or the coaching or something has gotten them across that line and they're willing to do something that's frightening. And they always say the same thing. I'm sure they say the same thing to you too, "Why didn't I do it earlier? Oh my god, I feel so good now."

# THE GROUND YOU'RE STANDING ON

## Episode #1014

### Tim Fulton, Vistage Georgia

**Tim Fulton:** There were a couple lessons that I got as a Chair that I try to share with new Chairs so that they can avoid all the mistakes that I made. As an example, Severin, I found as a Chair that I was only as good as the ground I was standing on. Meaning if I was not healthy, either mentally or physically, I could not be of help to my clients. If I was sick, if I was in a bad mood, if I'd had a fight with my best friend, if I was not on solid ground, I was not at my best.

And so, the lesson there was to always try to be on solid ground. Before a Vistage meeting, before a one-to-one meeting, before a coaching session, I had to take a quick evaluation. Where am I going into this meeting? How strong is the little piece of ground that I'm taking up? How strong is that?

That was one lesson I learned as a Chair early on: trust the group. While I was the Chair and largely responsible for how the group operated, how the meetings operated, there were times that I would do things just anticipating how the group would respond, and sometimes they would respond favorably, sometimes they wouldn't. And what I began to learn after a while was if I had a tough decision,

I would go to the group with that decision. Rather than make the decision myself, I would take it to the group and the group was always smarter than I was.

Hard to imagine! They were always smarter than I was.

And so, over time, I would just say, "Tim, I gotta trust the group on this one." I would go to the group, whether it was a member that maybe I was on the fence about, or maybe a change that we were going to make in the agenda or the way the meetings were being operated. Trust the group, I think is maybe some of the best advice that I can give to a new Chair.

# OPPORTUNITY IS NOWHERE

## Episode #1080

## Tony Lewis, Vistage Missouri

**Tony Lewis:** Questions are powerful, but silence is maybe more powerful in certain situations. The last thing you want to do is tell somebody what to do.

You observe.

I don't want to try to solve their problems. That's not my job as a facilitator or a coach. My job is to help them see through the clouds. If you're successful as a coach in getting them to see through the cloud that they're in, they will solve their own problem.

I used to have a saying up on my wall in my office at ConAgra and it said, *"Opportunity is nowhere."* People would come into the office, and they'd say, "I have this problem. What should I do?" I'd say, "Look at the sign" and they'd look at the sign. Most of them would say, "Opportunity is nowhere. What does that have to do with it?" I'd say, "Just concentrate and look at the sign and see what it's really saying." What it really said was "Opportunity is now here."

Once I could lead them to understanding that, then I could ask the right questions and usually they'd solve their own problem.

# THE POWER OF SILENCE

## Episode #1006

### Glenn Warring, Former Vistage Chair and Chair of ChairVoice

**Glenn Waring:** Well, sometimes I think my role is to be quiet and we're creating, if I can use the word, a 'sacred space.' It's the inexpressible, it's the 'mysterium' that occurs between two individuals that makes it strong.

I think most of the encounters I've had that felt like strength were grounded deeply in a moving experience, and that was certainly moving, that the loss of a child to a parent is always going to be profound and affect that parent for the rest of her life. Yeah, we didn't talk for quite a while there.

Sometimes in groups, I've come to the same number of minutes for silence and it's surprising to me. I got a little nervous the second time it happened. I looked at my watch and I said, "Well, I'm gonna wait as long as I did before." And right on the button, somebody spoke up and broke the silence. But the silence was so important for the group. They were weighing a very heavy problem in a hospital of all places. And the number you may ask is 22… total silence. The whole group of people, 22 minutes, and the meter's running, and it was a profound lift each time.

# PASSION, PURPOSE, CALLING

## Episode #1057

### Kevin McKeown, Vistage Washington

**Kevin McKeown:** It is lonely at the top and it's even lonely if you're not quite at the top. It can even be lonely for key executives, right? You don't have to be at the top to be lonely. If a peer group is structured in the right way, it is a great outlet to help you preserve your most important personal relationship.

**Severin Sorensen:** If you had to put a title on the story of your career of life, what would the title of that book be?

**Kevin McKeown:** It's *"The Ripple that Inspired a Thousand Positive Tsunamis."*

It's a great, great honor to be able to lead leaders. From my martial arts, it's bushido, the way of the peaceful warrior, right?

The other thing that I love about coaching and my best days whether it's a one-on-one, or it's a group setting, and I'm asking tough questions that are just probing and penetrating. I'm like, "Are you okay?" And my member would say, and he or she would look at me and go, "I know you really care." And so, I always try to ask, "Hey, how did we do today?" You know, "How did I show up for you? What was most impactful about this?" "Those are really tough questions, Kevin, but I know you care." That's what I want to be remembered for, is that this is a guy that not just cares, but you've got to build relationships to care. Right?

**Severin Sorensen:** Yeah. I love that.

**Kevin McKeown:** I'm very lucky because you know that if I focus on my energy, and if I know how to take care of myself emotionally, it allows me to do this work, which is passion, purpose, calling. And when you're allowed to do work, that's truly passion, purpose, calling, I think that life is just better. Life is sweeter. There's just more joy.

I hope that I can be a beacon for other people to really delve into what it means to actually pursue something that's passion, purpose, calling; the intersection of those three things.

Keepers of the Flame 2010

# WHAT'S IN YOUR WAY?

## Episode #1002

## Ozzie Gontang, Former Chair of 34 Years and Cope Award Winner from California

**Severin Sorensen:** Can you share with me a few thoughts on your Vistage experience?

**Ozzie Gontang:** It was basically 34 years. Till my dying day, I will honor Vistage and TEC for what they gave me and all of the men and women of Vistage, all of the chairs, because of that ability that gave me the opportunity to give because I received so much.

And again, what I said early on when I first started, it was having those mentors, that collegial spirit, that what I have, I will give you whatever it is that will be of help to you. And at the same time, with that, came

Ozzie Gontang and Bob Nourse
at 30th TEC Anniversary

the challenging questions from my peers of, "What's getting in your way?" And so that introspection of looking at what is it that is stopping me because of my own mindsets, or self-limiting beliefs, or the imposter syndrome, all of those things. It was a gift of each of those individuals in my life. And again, creating the relationship with them! They're all my friends and they will always be my friends until my last breath.

## In Closing...

What can one say about the chairs of Vistage other than "wow?"

Readers and listeners now have a taste of what it's like to be a Chair in Vistage and the care and attention they put into their craft as a coach, mentor, and facilitator of Vistage peer executive groups. The Vistage Chairs that I have met during my affiliation with TEC-Vistage are some of the brightest, most resourceful, caring, kind, intelligent, lifetime learning, and serviceable people that I know. For most Chairs, the labor is a work of passion, it is a calling, and you heard as much in their comments in these podcast excerpts.

To conclude, in this episode review, we celebrated Vistage's 65th anniversary by exploring the early roots of its founder, Bob Nourse, and we cross-walked through the early foundations of the organization and its purpose. We also explored the role of the Vistage Chair, the executive coach that serves three functions: coach, mentor, and peer group facilitator.

TEC-Vistage is recognized as the pioneer of these types of mentoring mastermind groups. Vistage differentiates itself from other business-focused self-help assemblies by providing professional facilitation from an executive coach called a Chair, who has had significant prior business experience and deep training in coaching skills and executive peer group facilitation. The Vistage Chair's role is to facilitate the peer group discussions, asking questions to draw out the expertise of the group members experiences and ideas, and periodically provide expert advice and guidance to the members when asked, while fostering a culture of trust, confidentiality, and open communication among the members.

Keepers of the Flame 2011

The goal of the Chair in this model is to help members gain new perspectives, solve problems, and make better decisions by sharing their experiences and learning from one another.

The Vistage organization has undergone several changes over the years to adapt to the evolving needs of members and the business environment. Vistage continues to serve the small to medium-sized companies, and over the years a number of these companies have become quite large. There are now a great number of multi-generational Vistage member companies with parent-to-child handoff of business responsibilities, wherein the next generation receives coaching, training, and supportive peer group work to shepherd the family-owned businesses through the next generations.

On this note, I've had the opportunity to work with several, 3 and 4-generation Vistage member companies, and what Vistage has done for these corporations and the business owner families is extraordinary.

In addition to expanding geographies to operate worldwide, Vistage has also expanded to serve different types of businesses and industries as well as nonprofits. Vistage now offers broad peer groups for a range of leadership levels from advancing and emerging leaders, up to the key executive and chief executive levels. Furthermore, Vistage has adapted to the digital age and now offers virtual peer advisor group meetings and webinars as well as online member communities to provide associates with access to resources and support regardless of their location.

I anticipate that Vistage will have a bright future as it continues to innovate and adapt to the changing needs of small and medium-sized businesses in years to come.

If you are an executive coach and found this topic interesting and wonder if you might be a good candidate for a Vistage Chair, I'd love to talk to you. I'm happy to share my own journey and help you navigate your own go or no-go decision to becoming a Chair. If it's the right decision for you, I'm happy to refer you into the organization to help you get your best start.

Being a Vistage Chair is truly one of my life's greatest honors. I'm happy to share my personal journey with others to help them make the decision if they think this is the right path for them. You can reach me at @SevSorensen on Twitter or Severin Sorensen on LinkedIn or at my website, ePraxis. That's epraxis.com.

# Quotes from the Vistage Chair Community

With each session on the podcast, we end with a few quotes for you to ponder, and our quotes today come from members of our Vistage Chair community that keep my mind flowing with imagination and curiosity.

First, from Carol Steinberg, she invites you as the executive to consider *"What kind of shadow are you casting?"* Be mindful of your shadow as a leader.

From Bud Carter when he quoted Michael Cammack, *"If you can't change the people, change the people."*

From Pat Murray, *"Great leaders seem to gain ground in conundrums others find impossible."*

From Cindy Hesterman, CEO of Vistage, Florida, and a recipient of the Red Scott Award. She offered this poem, *To Leave a Legacy* by Red Scott:

> *"How much better is it to give rather than receive? Service in any form is both generous and beautiful. To just give encouragement, to impart sympathy, to show interest, to banish fear, to build self-confidence, or to simply awaken some hope in the hearts of others. No greater service or gift can one give."*

So, until next time, be your best self, seek to uplift others, be good, and do good. This has been an Arete Coach review, celebrating the 65th anniversary of Vistage with author Severin Sorensen.

### # # #

Since the time of producing my original podcast on the history of TEC-Vistage and the legacy of Bob Nourse, I've had the wonderful opportunity to speak to another former president of TEC Wisconsin, Jim Handy. With Jim, I got into the history and further color analysis of Bob Nourse, who he was, what he strived to achieve, and this legacy we call TEC-Vistage. Here now in its entirety is our conversation relayed in Arete Coach Podcast 1123.

This discussion was one of my favorites, and truly highlights so much of the history and power behind Vistage, and everything we stand for. I know you will gain so many insights into coaching, as well as how we got to where we are.

Enjoy!

# YESTERDAY & TOMORROW

## Episode #1123

### Jim Handy, Former President of TEC Wisconsin

**Severin Sorensen:** This is the Arete Coach Podcast with Severin Sorensen and his guest Jim Handy. Jim is an executive coach, mentor, business advisor, trainer, and former President of TEC Wisconsin. This interview was recorded on March 9th, 2023, via Zoom video.

You are listening to Severin Sorensen, executive coach and curator of the Arete Coach Podcast, where we explore excellence in the art and science of executive coaching. Today I had the pleasure of speaking with Jim Handy, an accomplished executive coach, mentor, business advisor, and former President of TEC Wisconsin, with a notable track record that includes successfully launching and managing two businesses, as well as a business consulting practice focused on strategic planning, organizational alignment for growth, and family business succession. Jim has

Jim Handy, Former President TEC Wisconsin

worked with countless CEOs and managers across a diverse range of industries.

Additionally, he has served on the board of directors for various businesses and nonprofit organizations. As a volunteer business mentor for SCORE for over 10 years, Jim has also demonstrated a deep commitment to helping entrepreneurs and small business owners achieve their goals. His expertise spans business startup and growth, strategic planning, operations, sales, organizational design and alignment, consulting practice, and membership-based business models.

Given Jim's impressive career and wealth of experience as an executive coach, mentor, advisor, and leader in the executive peer group industry, I knew he would be an exceptional guest for today's episode of the Arete Coach Podcast.

So welcome, Jim.

**Jim Handy:** Thank you.

**Severin Sorensen:** I'm excited to have you here. So, you are an interesting one... I find your name throughout history, particularly of TEC and Vistage, but when I try to go back online, you're like this mystery man. So perhaps you can take me back. In the early days of your career, how did your feet take you into executive coaching and peer group facilitation?

**Jim Handy:** After school with a major in economics and minor in psychology, I went into business with a large corporation in Minneapolis. And after a few years, I felt at that time it wasn't for me. Retrospect, it may have been, but at the time I didn't, and they brought in a consultant to do some planning and some other things. He was involved in the human potential movement. I became intrigued, and he really became a mentor of mine. I was probably 26 or 27 at the time. And as a result of that relationship, I left the corporate world, and I went back to school to work on a graduate degree mostly because I could get the G.I. bill and feed my wife and two kids.

The consultant and I had contact there as a result of that. And he also was a speaker, a resource specialist for Bob Nourse at TEC. And when Frank Sterner, the first person that Bob brought on, was leaving, Bob put out a letter to I'm sure many different people, but one was for resource specialist, if members knew anyone. And my mentor, David Jones, he told me about it. And so, I met with Bob and we ended up working out. I came to move from Minnesota to Milwaukee. I took over the two groups that Frank Sterner was running and he went back to be a, I believe he was a dean, but anyway, he was at the Krannert School of Management at Purdue.

**Severin Sorensen:** Let me take you back. You said you went to college on a G.I. Bill. What service were you in?

**Jim Handy:** I was in the Army Security Agency.

**Severin Sorensen:** It's amazing how many veterans are in the TEC Vistage community. I always like to go back and celebrate and thank people for their service. So, thank you for that.

And it's great that you were able to get your graduate degree.

**Jim Handy:** I didn't end up getting the degree. As it turned out I moved, it was in a smaller town like the one I was raised in, so I knew how to live there without much money. And it was Mankato State University now, but at the time they were a teacher's college, and it was a brand-new program called Experiential Education. Amazingly, at the time, it was heavily influenced by the human potential kinds of things; of groups, peers learning from peers, learning by doing. I don't know if there are other degrees that would fit being a TEC Chair more, but coincidentally it fit very well.

**Severin Sorensen:** Let's talk about that human potential movement. You and I were talking before the podcast began and I put together an episode celebrating 65 years of TEC Vistage and

Keepers of the Flame 2012

really going back to the early days. And it was interesting in so many individual's recollections of that moment, how important the readiness for peer group type work and the human potential movement was.

I was not there at that time. You were. Can you take us back and what was it like? What was happening on campuses? What was this learning like? Because I know that Bob Nourse actually got involved in something called Cambridge House as well. I don't know if that was one of the ones that you were involved in but take us back to that time because that's something that not everyone would be aware of.

**Jim Handy:** Yes. And I later became involved with Cambridge House too; not at the level of Bob. But there were various pockets of the movement. There was Levine out of the East Coast, and he's started the encounter kind of group movement. And that's where my mentor was. He was conducting encounter groups, where people would go, and you talk about peer-centered groups. You just start out and there is no structure whatsoever. And the whole idea is people become frustrated. It's over a weekend and they become frustrated, and they're kept up late. And pretty soon it breaks down and the idea is you rebuild back.

There was also Fritz Pearls in Canada and then a big influence obviously out of Wisconsin was Carl Rogers and group-centered leadership. And there were a lot of different pockets in a lot of different organizations like Cambridge House were doing things, doing workshops and so forth that were self-discovery kinds of things. They were all over the place. And for some reason, the contacts I had with it, the Episcopal Church seemed to have a lot to do with it. Not officially, but that's where a lot of it happened. In fact, my mentor was a former Episcopal priest, so there were pockets of it all over.

The idea of course was great. If we can use these psychological tools to make people that are not well, well, think how much we could do with people that are well! And I think we're starting to run into trouble. And I know, again, my mentor David Jones was involved in it, was trying to get some sense of credibility. They struggle with that, and anybody could hang out a shingle. So, they had people doing encounter groups and sensitivity training was the word I was trying to think of. They were doing things like that and weren't really qualified for it, and it was sketchy. So, it didn't go away. It faded into other parts. It faded into business practices. It faded into education. It faded into other areas.

**Severin Sorensen:** Okay. As you were talking about that, I was going back and looking with the capable assistance of Amelia Chatterley, the instance I call ChatGPT. When you mentioned Levine, particularly in these early encounter groups, what is mentioned there is Arnold Mindell Levine, who was known as Arnold Mindell. He was a psychotherapist and author who played a significant role in the encounter groups. He also trained with Carl Rogers; somebody you've mentioned who was deeply influenced by his work. And Mindell also brought his own unique perspective to the field, drawing on his background in physics and his interest in Jungian psychology. So, it's interesting going back and looking at their early approach.

But as you mentioned it, it was early. It represented something new. There are many times when people can feel, sense something, and you get lots of different inroads to it. You mentioned that it started taking some interest, let's say, in some of the business fields. You mentioned I think in Bob's history as well, you see the Episcopalian Church, but more religious involvement of such groups. So, summarize that period. How did you grow from that period into where some of these concepts made their way into kind of peer group you work with.

**Jim Handy:** My mentor, David, was in a business situation where he used a lot of those concepts. It was, quote, 'planning,' but it was using those concepts. And then in the graduate work that I was doing, it was studying those kinds of things and practicing them. And then really it was when I got to Milwaukee and worked with Bob. I didn't go there because of the human potential movement. I went there because I was very interested in the idea of the peer learning with the groups and the group-centered, group leadership of the groups. So that's where I got more involved with it. But I was never as deep into it as Bob Nourse.

**Severin Sorensen:** So, when you say he was deep into it, I know that he really got into it intellectually, started learning and started participating. What was it you recall about Bob in that period that helped him in terms of his early framing of what he was trying to do with this TEC movement at the time?

**Jim Handy:** Part of this is history again. Bob started in 1957, as you've mentioned, in October with that first group. Which, by the way, I believe is still running. It was a few years ago. And I joined him in 1973. Frank Sterner was the first one, and he joined him in a group, something like 1967 when Bob was in his early sixties and wanted to be sure that TEC went beyond him.

**Severin Sorensen:** Take me back to 1973. At that point, you're looking at about 16 years or so of experience. Did you have any idea then that this Vistage would be what it is today from those early days?

**Jim Handy:** Not at all.

I shouldn't say "not at all."

Again, Bob really wanted this to develop beyond him. And so, bringing Frank Sterner in who was... let me digress a second also and talk about, I don't know if people realized the impact that Purdue's Krannert School of Management had on the future of TEC. Frank Sterner came from there, and I imagine in the beginning he was a resource specialist and he joined Bob for about five years.

During that time, he brought in another resource specialist from Purdue named Fred Cheney, and Fred became involved. And then he entered a licensing agreement with Bob Nourse where he and Bill Hall went out to California to start the groups. And their license agreement was really based on growth. And I have not seen it, but as I understand it, they were to have 10 groups in 10 years in 10 cities. Growth was in their DNA when they started. And then in terms of Krannert, Harry Dennis was a student there and he heard about TEC. Harry Dennis, also a doctorate, came from Purdue at Krannert. So, the three main people, the first chair after Bob, and the people who ended up running the two, one in Milwaukee, Harry Dennis, and Fred Cheney, all came from Krannert School. So, when I came in it was fairly well established the model and so forth. And I was given the groups TEC 5 and TEC 6 that Frank had started, and I took those over. 6 months later, Harry Dennis came in and joined us and he started a group in Madison, and from there we started to grow.

**Severin Sorensen:** At that time, you were... obviously early days, different structures than today, but at that time, if you were the President of the organization, you were also actively serving as a Chair?

**Jim Handy:** Yes.

**Severin Sorensen:** So, you had multiple duties. That's interesting. When you came in, how many groups were there in 1973 that you recall?

**Jim Handy:** We had 5 in Wisconsin, in Milwaukee. And I'm not sure, but I think it was about the same in California. And Fred was experimenting with what the relationship would be. Now it's clear cut. Chairs come in and they have groups, they start groups, and run groups and there's a certain commission base and so forth. At that time, everybody was experimenting with how to do that. Are they part owners of the group? Do they do this and that? So, I think there were about 10 total sets.

**Severin Sorensen:** Okay. I won't fact check you on that since I can't find any of the facts, but it's wonderful. This is the cool part about history.

I think of some of the work we're doing more like a PBS special where we're going back and talking to people who were aware in those days. Because it's just so interesting to look at the nuance and you never know how things go, but it's interesting some of those early steps, how the steps might have been put into soft soil, but they've hardened over and that became directional in terms of the way the organization moved forward.

**Jim Handy:** Yes. There's one more thing, if I might add to that...

**Severin Sorensen:** Sure.

**Jim Handy:** Was the climate. And by the way Harry and I bought the business from Bob, I'm guessing must have been about 1977 or so as Bob didn't retire at that point. So that's when I became President or Harry. We switched off every year. We were equal.

But also, there was a period of time, and I want to say it was the late seventies into the early eighties, where peer groups went from, "You're kidding, you actually let people into your plant?"

Keepers of the Flame 2013

which they would've said in the fifties, it became a very hot item. And I'd always surmised not knowing if there is any truth to this or not, that it has something to do with The Nummi plant in California, and Tokyo and the Japanese being open to General Motors and all those people. I don't know what it was, but all of a sudden you just put out a flier and for an informational meeting and we'd get 30, 40, 50 people to come learn about it.

There was a period of years there where it did really grow. We just happened to be positioned right. We were in the right place, and it caught a wave.

**Sorensen:** Yeah, as I look at what was going on at Harvard Business School at the time and the work of say, Toyota Motors and Kaizen and the Kanban and different types of innovations in this interest of really applying information science or management science to these processes, it certainly was important. And you see a lot of business schools that started up at that time as well.

**Jim Handy:** Interestingly, Bob one time went back for the early groups and the majority of the groups began in a down economic period, which makes sense. That's the time everyone has a question about how do you do this CEO thing?

**Severin Sorensen:** That's interesting too, because that was my experience when I started chairing in 2010 and I had a wonderful time, but it was right in the throes of the rebuild and people were stuck, and businesses were stuck. And I was thinking, "What a great time, because now they need it." If anybody's thinking about starting a group, this is a wonderful time. Now, as people get anxious about recessions and that should be a growth phase for any practice.

**Jim Handy:** We're learning that here now in another organization. Yeah.

**Severin Sorensen:** That's great. It's fun to talk about those times. It's hard today to talk about because we have the hindsight of history. We know what happened. But at that time, as you were thinking and growing, one of the hardest parts that I find that people have is how do you get beyond the Renaissance man or woman in the Chair model? In other words, for the model to work, you must have someone who is great at pulling people in and also great at doing the work. And it's like you find people on the other side, but very few can do both successfully.

**Jim Handy:** Yes. That is really interesting. And we had a very eclectic group as we started expanding in Milwaukee. I think maybe California too. But in the beginning, we weren't all that interested in finding businesspeople. Partly because we couldn't afford to pay anybody that was good enough to be a Chair. They had been used to making more. So, we brought in people from academia. We brought in people who had been social therapists and really understood group dynamics. And if I had to put my money on a group, I would go there first. They could learn the business jargon. We had some senior naval officers, a couple of them.

So, we had an eclectic group.

And what we did when we hired them, we called it 'Running the Gauntlet.' This was early years. We had maybe as we grew, 8, 9, 10 of us and anybody that wanted to be a chair went down and talked to everyone. And some of them, by the time they got halfway through, didn't even want to talk to anybody anymore. But those that went all the way through the group itself, our group had a sense of, 'Yeah, they're gonna work.' And we really did have a very good hit rate.

**Severin Sorensen:** When you say you had to talk to everyone, are they talking to Chairs or are they talking to all the members?

**Jim Handy:** No. Chairs.

**Severin Sorensen:** Okay.

**Jim Handy:** There would be some interviews with a member or two that we trusted, yes, but primarily it was the Chairs. And then in those days we did group marketing. While the Chair was responsible, they were responsible for following up on leads. And again, this is a time where you could get leads. It wasn't quite so, I think, difficult as it is today. They would follow up and we would have steps and we knew in 90 days if they were going to be successful or not. They might not have a full group, but we knew they were going to make it. In the early days, the group was 6 to 8 people when Bob started it and then went to 8 to 10 and 10 to 12 and so on. So, it was interesting. I know with a few of them, I couldn't use the word "sell." You, I had to say, "Go tell them to join." They could do that, but they couldn't sell. The idea of selling was, from their background, didn't feel like they were selling.

**Severin Sorensen:** It's still bristles as well. No one wants to feel like you're selling a commodity, like your garage door, this is something special that you're invited into.

**Jim Handy:** Yes, exactly. But the good ones always had a waiting list. We had one, Rex Coryell, and we always laughed. The Chairs followed him around like seagulls around a garbage scow, because he always had more prospects than he could take in his group. Oftentimes in his groups, others would interview. I don't know if they still do that today, they didn't necessarily have a final 'yes' or 'no,' but they would meet the prospect maybe at breakfast before a TEC meeting, something like that.

**Severin Sorensen:** Yeah. I think the best Chairs continue to do that. I know that was part of my practice as well, is get them introduced. I would come to a meeting, and I would say, "All right, we've got the following people. Who would like to interview them?" I'd get two volunteers and say, "I need you to take them to breakfast or lunch. Find out more about them. If you think they're a great fit, friendship them. If not, come back and let us know. It's got to fit the culture of the group."

It's a good practice. We want to look at their club-ability. How well do they fit the club?

**Jim Handy:** Exactly.

**Severin Sorensen:** As opposed to hit them with the club.

**Jim Handy:** Yeah.

**Severin Sorensen:** That's an interesting process. All right, so you had an opportunity to be a Chair.

Tell me what your early days of chairing were like. You had those two groups. Did you grow any of your own groups or did you just manage the ones that were there?

**Jim Handy:** As it turns out, I did not. I had the ones that I was there, and then we had a rouge group out of Chicago. Somebody exactly the same model. I took that one, and then later I took over one of Bob's. I always thought that was something that I missed, not starting one, but my first experience was first of all learning from Bob. And if I could just talk a bit about that…

**Severin Sorensen:** Please.

**Jim Handy:** Yeah. Bob, first of all, Bob didn't…We all did TEC. We all did chair. He didn't do chair, he didn't do TEC. He *was*

Keepers of the Flame 2014

Chair. Every relationship I saw him in, he was a Chair. It was a space with a lot of silence and a few questions and other focuses. And he did it when he sold.

I went on a selling, calling with him. One time early on when I was first there and the CEO said, "I've got 10 minutes. What do you gotta tell me about TEC?" And Bob asked him a few questions, and I am not exaggerating, it was like 45 minutes later we're touring his plant. And then he said, "Tell me about this TEC." And Bob said, "We've got plenty of time to talk about TEC later." I couldn't believe it. And he often said himself that it was just almost lightning strike that he founded this thing.

He went out on his property, as you probably know, one Saturday morning and put it all together after all the input that he had. And he often would tell me that, he said, "That's probably the only creative thing I ever did!" And I always believed that people like Bob, aren't, you know, it's more of the consultants and the marketing people and folks and trainers that might go out and do this.

He did it, and I don't think anybody else could've done it and it would've been the same.

Bob & Gracie Nourse

So, I think it was almost a lightning striking. I'm getting a little esoteric there, but just watching Bob and learning from Bob and how he did it and how he opened up. When I was training chairs, I would call, talk about the 'CEO Blind Spot' that we've all got. Nobody tells us we have spinach in our teeth, or the tie doesn't match the shirt. But the CEO is huge and everybody that works around him obviously knows where the edge of that is, but the CEO doesn't. And Bob was just a master of not only going inside of that, but taking the group to open up so that there was that trust and a level of feedback and exchange inside that circle. They weren't getting it anywhere else, if that makes any sense.

**Severin Sorensen:** It does.

**Jim Handy:** And that was probably my biggest learning, and being an extrovert, my biggest challenge from Bob.

**Severin Sorensen:** That's great. If you think about yourself and your first year of Chairing, and then you think of yourself later on in Chairing, what did you learn later on that you wish you had learned in that first year?

**Jim Handy:** It sounds strange, but off the top of my head, I'd say probably that it isn't as complicated as I thought it was in the beginning. If you trust the dynamics and stick to them, they'll take care of it, if that makes sense.

**Severin Sorensen:** And let's talk about the dynamics. What are the dynamics of the group?

**Jim Handy:** Again, the questions, letting silence work. Back then we had smaller groups. You might end up with a group of 3 or 4 sometimes at a meeting. And this I learned from Bob, he'd just rub his hands and say, "What a great opportunity we have to go deep!" Learning to trust those kinds of things.

My relationships tended to be stronger with the facilitator, with the Chairs. They're the ones that I got to know and groomed and hired and recruited over time and trained and worked with. As I look back, what I walked away with was this magical model of the TEC peer group and the facilitators. And I watched so many individuals come in mid-career not liking where they were and making that change and just blossoming. People, just brilliant people. One came from Marquette. He was in the theology department. He just flowered and went into a whole new career, and he was writing books.

**Severin Sorensen:** Talk to me about your transition. So, you're in, you grew for a period of time, at what point did you say, "It's time for me to do my next thing?"

**Jim Handy:** Primarily it was personal, the reasons that I sold my interest in TEC at the time. It had nothing to do with TEC. That wasn't personal about TEC. It was outside of TEC and in retrospect, not real bright...not real smart.

And then I had the wherewithal to do that because we licensed them all, but 5 states of the country to California. We then reached an agreement where we would develop some of the states that we licensed them, and we developed those and then we did Minnesota, and we went into Philadelphia and Cleveland and so forth. And then we sold that back to California, and then I sold my half of the interest to Harry. So that gave me a fun base to do some of the things I wanted to do. So that's how I left.

And then I played around for a couple of years and did a little investing, but it wasn't a thrill. And then I started the Pernett Group, which again, was peer exchange and networking, but it wasn't CEOs. And this was the time when businesses, particularly our TEC level, if you will, businesses that are mid-sized or smaller, were catching up to all the quality movements; the ISOs and the world-class manufacturer, the lean manufacturing and all this. They now had to do that for their suppliers who were down the road. This put manufacturers together where they went to each other's plant and learned from each other, everything from ISO, and we had special groups for ISO and Kanban, and also leadership.

So, I started that business and I set it up. I didn't really get that involved in the operation, just set it up. And I owned that for about 10 years. And then I sold that, and that's still running. Then I retired, moved to Minneapolis, and I got involved in SCORE. And now this new group MBMentors.org in Minneapolis and its strong emphasis on roundtables.

**Severin Sorensen:** They are nonprofit, correct?

**Jim Handy:** Nonprofit and volunteer. We're all volunteer, and we really are OEMs like the counties and the chambers and people, and they have funds and monies to do this for typically stage-two to stage-three businesses.

**Severin Sorensen:** It's great to be able to give back because the wisdom is there. Some people just don't have the budget or the organization. I'm sure a lot of people get these requests: "Would you consider coaching here? Coaching there?" And I look at it, I'm like, "Yeah, you probably need coaching. But I don't see the model." It doesn't fit where I am. But it's wonderful that there are resources for others out there. And I think SCORE does some good work as well, trying to make things accessible and it's really good for entrepreneurs trying to think, "Should I roll into this area?" and having a mentor help them.

Tell us about your time with SCORE.

**Jim Handy:** I was with SCORE, it must have been 8-10 years, mostly mentoring, coaching one-on-one. So, I did that. I also did workshops, planning, and some general ones for startups and businesses. And then we did start groups.

**Severin Sorensen:** I want to go back to something you said just a conversation before this, when you had your group, and you had this company you called Pernett Group?

**Jim Handy:** Yes, PernettGroup.com.

**Severin Sorensen:** And you went out to do factory visits. That's an interesting thing to me. Talk to me about that. How did you set them up? What did you learn? What were you trying to discover? What kind of groups got to do that?

**Jim Handy:** Companies that joined knew that part of their responsibility was to share. So, we would set up meetings at various businesses. We had, for example, some of the bigger ones, Johnson Control, Harley Davidson, and they were very generous. But also, some smaller ones that were really doing great things. We went into one, for example, and this was a smaller business, but they talked about how they took a line with 12 people on the line, and they said, they told the people on the line, "You take it down to 4 people running it, and you let us know what you need for equipment and machinery and we will not lay anyone off." So, we would have teams come in there and they'd meet their manufacturing managers and whoever was involved, engineers, whatever, would learn from that company how they did that. And they would talk to the workers and what they liked about it or didn't like. So it was that kind of exchange. And then there were small groups of manufacturing managers and then small groups we call Special Interest Groups. The people who were managing the installation of ISO back there in the nineties, and we would have groups there. So, there was very little CEO involvement, which we made sure we didn't do. It wasn't just non-compete. It's something I wouldn't do to either TEC or Harry Dennis. And so, it's still going, as I say, and it grew in Wisconsin and Illinois.

Does that answer your question?

**Severin Sorensen:** Yeah, it does. It's interesting to me. I had some very successful entrepreneurs come to me and they were talking about what they wanted to do. They really wanted to do these factory tours, and that was something that was important to them.

For example, Zappos had a program where you could come and look at their culture and you could go to Tesla, or you could go to other places and really learn different parts of what they're doing. And so that's a great experiential-type learning that one might do. And I was always fascinated by those possibilities and what one could learn. Doing these little charrettes, if you will, "Learn this, learn that. What do you take away?" Broadening out the opportunities for learning.

**Jim Handy:** And it also built networks that they were all encouraged and did call back and say, "We ran through your plant. What has happened here?" "I've got a guy." "Yes. Send him over." Yeah, it was great!"

**Severin Sorensen:** That's very helpful. Thank you for that. How has your experience and learning shaped your views of business and coaching today?

**Jim Handy:** A couple ways. One when I started with TEC, I did not know what a business model was. And ever since then, I've been trying to find one nicer than TEC or Vistage.

I can't find one.

As I left, there's a lot of changes going on and how things are done. Obviously, technically we're starting to see things merge. The idea of mentor and coach and consultants, facilitators all starting to come together and that. But the one thing that seems to stick is that

Keepers of the Flame 2015

with the CEOs is that the role of CEO is still very developmental, if you will. I know that's a good word, but you're a new CEO and you go through all the new people, and if you're a family business, you're working with dad's people who don't know you, and you realize Dad knew more about what they were doing than they did and all of that. And you mature through it all where you're at the other end and you're looking at succession and how you get out. And those things don't change. They're very human, developmentally. So, there'll be a lot of different ways that goes on.

But I find if I go back to that, if I just go right back to what's going on inside the experience of these people, either as individuals or as a group, it's probably like working with adolescents. Adolescents are adolescents, regardless of whether they're on screen or they were painting outhouses, it doesn't make any difference.

I don't know if that speaks to your question.

**Severin Sorensen:** You bring up an interesting metaphor here. Why is it that in parenting we have to learn all the lessons and then once we've learned them (you're thankful probably you're not having any more children at some point), but the idea is now we're expert at this or have some confidence, but then we're not doing it again. I see the CEO journey the same way.

**Jim Handy:** Yes.

**Severin Sorensen:** Unless they become a serial CEO, they have to learn all these lessons, but by the time they've had the hard corners knocked off and the rough edges smoothed, unless they go into mentoring, there's not a lot of opportunities for them to do those things again.

**Jim Handy:** Yes. And going back to the parenting too, once you know it, you can't explain it to your young parent-children any more than in business when Dad's out and now his daughter or son is in the presidency, and they aren't listening to him then either.

**Severin Sorensen:** Yeah.

**Jim Handy:** It's developmental and that is the constant. If I don't get too far away from that, I'm okay. If I don't get too cute with all the different angles and techniques and theories and concepts and so forth, I'm okay.

**Severin Sorensen:** Yeah. I released that podcast on the 65th anniversary. You mentioned you had an opportunity to hear it. Just curious, how did what you hear resonate with what you experienced then? Were we on track or were we off track with what was put on that message?

**Jim Handy:** I thought you were very on track. You knew more about the details than I could remember about Bob and Midland and so forth. There are some elements, I think we've talked a little bit about them today, that are just inside feelings having been there. But I thought it was right there.

**Severin Sorensen:** That was fun to look and listen and learn and try to put some sense to it. The other part that was interesting is, you talked about these different kinds of movements and things that were happening. And so, in thinking about the human potential movement, it gave me some curiosity to dig deeper into what was going on and go and look at the work of Maslow and Jung and others and think, "How did what was happening mold into the molecules of thought?" if you will. One electron hits another and we have these mashups of experience. I think we continue to learn. But I think what's so cool is that there was something happened there at a state that's largely stayed the same. There have been some improvements. Technology helps things sometimes. But the group is still there.

**Jim Handy:** Yes,

**Severin Sorensen:** There's still a chair. You had resources come in. That's still a part of the model.

**Jim Handy:** Yeah. If I might, a couple of things with Bob Nourse: he was a master at finding resource specialists, and of course he was the only one doing it. He always had this rule that he had to hear about them from three different sources before he'd bring them in. And the reason he called them 'resource specialists' is for the most part they weren't speakers. He was uncanny at bringing in high-end CEOs that I believe were just intrigued with the idea that he had this little group of CEOs.

**Severin Sorensen:** That's awesome.

**Jim Handy:** Oh, another thing; you mentioned notes. Just let me throw this in because I don't know if they exist anymore. Bob Nourse took copious notes of every one-on-one he did, and every meeting he ever did, and he put them in identical black little binders about four by six or something. And they were in a box, and they were all the years that he had done TEC. It was amazing history. And I had the box at home and then when I sold it, I gave it to Harry. And I've often thought I'd sure love to get my hands just to review that. Have you ever heard of that?

**Severin Sorensen:** I have heard that he took a lot of notes. I've not seen that box. One time Bob was describing what was happening, and you could tell he took copious notes because he described an actual conversation that took place, and he was describing the value of the group. And what the cool part is, the notes that he had taken would describe for anyone trying to be a Chair how you take apart an issue, how you ask deeper questions. And he takes it through, and then what do we find? The question you think you're asking is not the most important question. You strip away what the underpinnings are, and now you can really go after the most important things. And that was all there very early on. Just detailed as an issue.

Keepers of the Flame 2016

You know, there are books that people who've come into TEC or Vistage have written about their experience. I think there's one called *A Group*, and others where they describe some of the same experience, but none of the ones that I have read since that time go any better, if you will, to the granularity that Bob was able to do in that first group and actually demonstrate.

Now, I don't know if the early Chairs were able to see that script or that's how he would train them. One of the notes I looked at, he had written a journal at some point; a biography of his life. And it's in that biography where he gives an example in one of the chapters that kind of goes over that. And so that was interesting to see.

**Jim Handy:** Yes. And that might be an example of what I meant, where he didn't talk about or do TEC.

He *was* TEC.

You could feel it when he talked about it. And the biggest thing that I learned there, and have learned since, was the whole idea of question, silence, question, silence. I have bookoo records of questions for different situations. So, I became obsessed, and I learned that from him.

**Severin Sorensen:** Silence is wonderful, isn't it?

**Jim Handy:** Yes. I have to work at it, but it's wonderful.

**Severin Sorensen:** I truly have to work at it too. Sometimes I'm sitting on my hands or doing anything else. Just don't ruin a great moment!

Now, let's talk about Bob Nourse, particularly in terms of statements or sayings. What were some Nourse-isms, if you will; things that he would say that you remember to this day?

**Jim Handy:** One was the low-keyness. TEC had zero professional promotional material for the first 20 years or so, or, 18, 20 years. There was no brochure, there was no anything. It was all word of mouth. It was all referral. And he would teach me. I was used to him saying, "Okay, you're going to write to a CEO." You would write a nice formal letter back in those days in triplet and have it typed and all that kind of stuff.

He said, "Write a personal note. And when you're talking to these people, it's like you are asking them to play a game of golf. When you join this, you begin that relationship. You're not selling up, you're not selling down, you have that relationship."

Now, those are all my words, but that's the kind of message he left me with.

**Severin Sorensen:** All right. Let's go to this. You hit one of my passions of life: golf. I have an episode about business golf. It was recorded months ago, but I've saved it for that. But you brought this up, it's like you are asking them to play a round of golf. Tell me about that and how golf ties in; what that experience is in terms of how you introduced them to TEC Vistage?

**Jim Handy:** Mostly I guess it could have been tennis, which is really my sport. It was mostly the idea that you're slipping under the formality of business.

Because that's what TEC is about.

We're under all of that. We're deeper than that and we start out that way.

We start with a referral. Nobody's going to jump up and down because Jim Handy wrote him a note on a piece of paper, but if I mentioned Joe Hiles, who suggested I contact you, that's really what he was saying.

Even in the beginning of the relationship, it's as though we're inside of the noise, if you will. He didn't use those words. He would just say, "Simple and personal." But again, you learn mostly from Bob by watching Bob. Bob wasn't verbose. And oftentimes the things you'd learn from him, I think this is fair to say, would be in writing.

He wrote a thing called OCD; "Over the Chairman's Desk" for a while. It was a newsletter to all the members. He would bring it up and it'd be news about things that went on and maybe some discussions in the meeting, the group, building the community beyond the group; beyond all the groups.

But again, Bob and I were such different personalities that when I first started working for him, he made me quite nervous because I thought, "Ah, he is going to...whatever!"

One, you didn't get much feedback. And two, he's not judging me the way I wish, you know? So, I learned more from watching Bob, I think, and studying Bob than actually anything else.

**Severin Sorensen:** Your comment about being a different person, but the right person at the time, reminds me of the quote that you hear sometimes from Tao, *"When the student is ready, the teacher will appear."* And when you think about when the organization is ready, then you need the leader for the next stage. And it's the old, *"What got you here won't get you there."*

**Jim Handy:** Yeah.

**Severin Sorensen:** And you do need these different leaders. It reminds me a lot of the good work that Tom Foster does in terms of the Time Span Journeys, looking at Ichak Adizes' work of how you have leaders for different organizations, and I certainly recognize that for myself. There are certain stages there I'm really great at, but I'm not the billion-dollar CEO. That's somebody else. I might coach them, but there's a difference between coaching and doing. And I think that's really important to understand about oneself.

**Jim Handy:** I really agree. And in fact, even with the expansion of TEC, I, for whatever reason, had a three or four or five-state brain. That's what I thought. And we brought in another guy who was very influential by the name of Gary Bratland. And he worked with us and helped expand and he just amazed me. And then Fred and those guys had an international mind and I thought, "Dude, I just, I don't have that! How am I going to get to Australia and then Japan and then, I just, how do I get to Chicago?"

**Severin Sorensen:** So that's interesting. Was there a point where you mentally switched from, I'm a Chair and now I want to be a leader, or were you brought in to be a leader and that required being a Chair also?

**Jim Handy:** No, no. It was definitely a turning point as I became confident, and probably the biggest turning point, yeah.

Here's the turning point: when we changed from a practice to a business. Up until Harry had been there maybe a year, and I'd been there 18 months and we were definitely a practice, and we stayed a practice for another two or three years. By that I mean, we all did our work. We were on salary; it wasn't tied to commission in any way. And then at the end of the year, we would divide up whatever money was left over, we always were under.

When we first started to expand, I remember laying on a bed in Green Bay in the freezing cold, and I couldn't get our event speaker to come up with me. He was going to fly. And of course, the plane couldn't come in, and I'm thinking, "Well, I got three people coming from Wausau that aren't going to make it." And so, I thought, "I've got to expand this thing to get somebody else in Green Bay."

So, we decided to bring in other Chairs. And that if Harry and I could drop a group and then turn a group over to someone else and then grow two more groups, we could go back to making the same little money we were making.

And so that was the point really.

We moved from being a practice to a business, and then we had the business model. So, each group was almost like a printing press. It was a Capital-Eight piece of equipment. When they went up, they rarely went down. And so that's when we said, "Okay, that's what we're about." And that was probably the biggest turn. I don't know if that speaks to your question or not.

**Severin Sorensen:** The great part about a question is the answer you provide is the right answer. Talk to me about your observations now of where the coaching industry has grown.

Keepers of the Flame 2017

**Jim Handy:** I think just as it was a shock and a little bit weird when Bob put groups of company's CEOs together in somebody's plant, I think the same thing with executive coaching. At first it was "What? Is that like remedial learning?" And it became more and more not only acceptable, but the thing to do. And it seems to be spreading more and more.

I think back in the early days, and some people like Thayer who was a resource speaker for us, and Pat Murray, who I can only think was brilliant, somebody I groomed for a year trying to get him into being a Chair. So, I think that it's much more acceptable now, particularly with the peer groups.

It's fairly amazing how the integrity of a group is hard to beat up. It's hard to destroy. Get them together, and they almost won't let a facilitator try to lead it. They won't let the facilitator take over. I think it's very powerful and it's become, much more, not only acceptable, but very popular. It's become more popular and it's becoming a little more specialized, I think, where if I'm going to have a coach, I want a coach that's in my business. And we see that in our mentoring, both in SCORE and the organization I'm in now, where they say, "I would like somebody that's in this business!" We have to tell them, "You can get a lot of coaching before you get to that. You're not at the point where you need somebody in your business, but..."

**Severin Sorensen:** Yeah, there is a need for mentoring, clearly. But coaching doesn't necessarily mean you have to have experience in that area. In fact, it might be a handicap for you being a coach if you have experience in an area because you'll think, "Oh, when I was doing it this way guess what..." There's probably lots of other ways that could keep you ruddered, if you will.

**Jim Handy:** Yes. In fact, I was always intrigued with what I thought was one level of creativity in you take a CEO from one industry into another industry and he's doing what was normal over here. And he or she is very creative over here. And I think of, what is it, LG; they make cranes and booms? LGL something like that. Anyway, they were manufacturers of lifts and booms, and they brought someone in from the auto leasing business, the large truck leasing, and they changed the industry, wrapped it up, rolled it up.

**Severin Sorensen:** So yeah, new paradigms, definitely. If you're in need of change, having someone from a different industry come in could definitely open up a new paradigm area. That's interesting.

A question I always like to ask on a podcast is, who were you in your youth? In your youth, when was the earliest time that you did something to make money? And what was that job you did?

**Jim Handy:** You mean early?

**Severin Sorensen:** Like, did you have a paper route? Did you mow lawns? Did you shovel snow? What did you do to earn money as a kid?

**Jim Handy:** I think the paper route maybe is the first view of that, or Charlie's market down on the corner where they told me, "Put the mushy potatoes in the middle of the bag, not the bottom or the top."

The paper routes were where I knew that I was first going to be an entrepreneur. I didn't know what an entrepreneur was, but looking back, that's where I had a big, huge Sunday route. And then I also had a few dailies and I had to collect, and I hired neighborhood kids to collect for me for something like a Hershey bar and a Coke.

**Severin Sorensen:** All right. Time out. Stop right there! Okay. You just passed the tests. So, when I asked this question, it's always a two-part question. The first part is: what did you do? And then the second part in your youth, did you organize anybody underneath you to do the work? And that seems to be the thing.

It's funny that you would get them to go do that. It reminded me of my own years…when I was 11, there was heavy snow, and they didn't have snow blowers like we have today. And so, I would go around, and I noticed that I could get the sale, so I'd go to the door and knock, I would talk to the person in the house, "Hey, this snow's really heavy. Would you like me and the guys here to shovel it for you?" They would say, "Oh my gosh, that would be great! How much would that cost?" And I would give them a price.

Initially I did one or two. I went and got all these elementary school kids to come with me and say, "Hey, come on. Bring your shovels here, I'll pay you."

And then I noticed the entrepreneur's rule: one for you, one for you, oh, the rest for me!

I thought that habit started so early, but when you talk about it in your paper route, that's the same thing that Jack Daley did with his, with the Chicago Sun Times.

**Jim Handy:** Is that right?

**Severin Sorensen:** Very similar. Yeah.

**Jim Handy:** I used to always say, if it's worth doing, it's worth hiring somebody to get it done.

**Severin Sorensen:** Alright. There's a good one.

**Jim Handy:** What I usually meant by that on a little more serious basis is that I can hire two or three people and do a whole bunch more.

**Severin Sorensen:** Yes, exactly. All right, there's my new-ism for you, so that's great! I'm going to jot that down by the way. We'll come down here to, at the end, I always do quotes. I'm going to drop that down. It'll be my Jim Handy quote.

**Jim Handy:** I don't know if that's the one I want mom to see!

**Severin Sorensen:** What is a mantra from Jim Handy? Do you have a mantra?

I got one for you now, it's called, *"If it's worth doing, it's worth hiring somebody to get it done."*

**Jim Handy:** Yeah. Yeah. That may be because I always leverage even my volunteer work, even organizing tennis activities; leverage was always big, so it was always, "If you can't find someone to do it, find two people!" It's a lot easier to get two people than it is to get one. I don't know if that works in business, but it works in volunteering.

Keepers of the Flame 2018

**Severin Sorensen:** Yeah. Volunteering is such an interesting thing in terms of getting people to do things because you're not paying them.

**Jim Handy:** Yeah.

**Severin Sorensen:** When you're paying somebody, sometimes people will do work even though they don't like it because they have the need. What is your success in getting people to volunteer and actually follow through?

**Jim Handy:** I like to sneak up on them. I start out with...I never describe exactly what the job is and all this kind of stuff. I usually like to say, "Have you got a few minutes? I need your brain. Have you got an hour for lunch? I need your brain about something we're trying to do." And very often I'll say, "Do you know anybody that can help out?" And they'll say, "Yeah, I can help out."

So, I start out with just, "I need your brain, I need your thoughts," and give them the issue, the solution, whatever, give them the gap that we're trying to reach, and that really is it. And then build camaraderie around that.

I really would prefer to have two people. And people say, "Oh, you need one butt to kick!" and all that kind of stuff. That's not true, certainly in volunteering, because if I'm volunteering with somebody, I'm going to do my share and pull my part of the wagon. If I'm doing it myself, I might slide, but I'm not going to let that other person slide.

**Severin Sorensen:** It's hard to quit when your peers are telling you, "We need to be there!"

**Jim Handy:** Yes.

**Severin Sorensen:** Whereas if you've done it on your own, that's certainly something I would not have thought that initially in looking at that. That's a gem. Thank you.

**Jim Handy:** Yeah. And as I say, then you tap into their passion. Just, "I need your brain," and they come up with a solution. I say, "That sounds good. How would you do that?" And pretty soon they're doing it!

**Severin Sorensen:** I like that. What's the most powerful question you've ever asked somebody in a coaching session?

**Jim Handy:** Ah, probably something along the line of... it had to do with actually taking an action and making a decision. One is, "What is it you really want to do?" And from there I try to take them beyond what seemed to be an intellectual decision-making process to a gut feel and connect with that somewhat. If the reticent is, "What is the risk, and can you live with it?"

Who was the guy from Texas who told about the Abilene story?

**Severin Sorensen:** Oh, is that Jerry? Yep,

**Jim Handy:** Jerry. In a way, he was a mentor of mine when I was first starting to have a leadership role in TEC.

**Severin Sorensen:** Yeah. Every time I think of about that book, I'm taking the knife out of my back,

**Jim Handy:** yeah. He was a funny, dry talking Texas guy. He was great.

**Severin Sorensen:** Yeah, he's great. Road Abilene (and The Abilene Paradox). Yeah. I love it.

So, looking back on your journey as a coach, what is a lesson you've recently learned you wish you'd learned earlier on?

**Jim Handy:** Letting the process work. Don't get in the way. And sometimes I'll get in the way of it. And that has to do with letting the silences work and all the techniques we know. But at some level it has to do with time; it has to do with everything. But I'd say that's still the one that keeps just getting me and pushing me.

Keepers of the Flame 2019

**Severin Sorensen:** That's interesting. There's no microwave to cause faster growth.

**Jim Handy:** Yeah, exactly! And sometimes I'm thinking there is, and I gotta say, "No, there isn't!"

**Severin Sorensen:** Oh, I know. I've gotten in trouble sometimes before when you have a very short amount of time.

**Jim Handy:** Yeah.

**Severin Sorensen:** You're like, "To process this issue is going to take longer. If we start, we're going to have somebody not bound up from their wounds. And that's unfair to have them go out of this session." You have to think about the time it takes to do good work.

**Jim Handy:** Yeah, very much so. And along that line, I think also, in fact on Monday I'm teaching that to some facilitators and some coaches. And another big one is just always remember it's their solution. It's not *the* solution, it's not *your* solution, it's *their* solution and *their* way of doing it. And it may be completely different. So, help them come to that and examine it. That to me is a lot of the work.

**Severin Sorensen:** In the literature today, the ICF and others make a great distinction between mentoring, advising, and coaching. Do you draw distinctions between those? Do you have swim lanes that you practice in today in your own work, or are those not relevant?

**Jim Handy:** We don't do consulting where we go do something for someone. But when we're doing the mentoring, we do have people with great experience. They can move back and forth from mentoring to coaching. But again, being careful that you're not consulting, you're not telling them what to do, you're bringing them along. But yes, you can certainly use your expertise in doing that.

With the round table facilitators, we back away from that too. I always tell them that you may, as soon as somebody throws out an issue, you're probably sitting there with about four good responses in your stomach.

Sit on them, be the last one to say anything, and then do you really need to say it?

First of all, your job is to have the group say it, get it out of the group, that sort of thing. So, but they're there because the people here, unlike the people we started out with, the guy from the theology department, these people do have vast experience in business. It's a marriage of those two.

**Severin Sorensen:** I think that's helpful. A different question. This one's about being a business operator. What is a powerful learning you've had as a business operator, owner operator, that serves you today?

**Jim Handy:** Interestingly, it really goes back to the paper route a bit. First, my leadership tends to be about ideas. If I don't have a good idea, somehow there's nobody following me. So, it tends to be ideas. And then when they have a business situation or a situation where I've got people now coming into my circle, it's not getting too far out in front of them. I'm trying to say, "Get involvement, get it!" And I'm talking everything, but also just the culture; are people believing what I believe?

I've been known to have absolute truth and turn around and there was no one else that thought I did, so I need to back up and bring them along.

**Severin Sorensen:** If you're the band leader though, there better be a band right with you. Turn around "Oh, come on guys!"

**Jim Handy:** Yeah, that's exactly right.

**Severin Sorensen:** Is there an important failure in your life, a business failure particularly, that taught you something valuable?

**Jim Handy:** Sometimes I act too quickly and while I'm in the business, it's not too bad because I do have people that will pull me back and say, "What are you smoking over there?"

But the decision, for example, to leave TEC, a couple things like that. They were too quick. And it may be even I sometimes now, looking back over your life, I'm curious about what life would've been in a large corporation now that I know me better and I know my style and I know my leadership and how I would develop. And

Keepers of the Flame 2020

sometimes I'm wondering if I was too quick to leave that. So, probably those kinds of decisions that I think maybe were too quick.

Fortunately, probably because I avoided the risk of somethings, I really didn't try to do something in business that just didn't work. I didn't have a business that didn't fly. For whatever reason, I was just blessed and probably didn't try stuff that was very difficult.

**Severin Sorensen:** Years ago, I was thinking about when I started off and I was building a business and I had this idea of visions of sugar plums in my head. I was out raising capital and I remember raising capital and the company said, "We love you, we love the business. This is gonna be awesome. We're going to blah blah blah, but here's our proposal for you." And I was the CEO of my own little company at the time. "What you're doing is awesome. We are going to fund it. You are gonna be integral in it. We want you as this visionary. We're gonna bring a Harvard MBA to run this thing for you! How does it all sound?"

I can remember just how hollow and initially hurt I was. I felt like "What, I'm not gonna be the one?" They said "No." They said "What you have is a special talent to do what you're doing. And that is the thing that's that tip of the spear that we need out there. We can get anybody else to come in and run this thing and that's what they're gonna do. So, you can do what you need to do, but no, we're not going to run this if you want to run it the same small way that you've been running things."

It was really interesting for me to understand what I do well and what others do well. And so, I've had a number of requests to take over the presidency of another company. Like, "You know all our issues." Yes, I do, but I'm your coach. I'm not your CEO. I go, "You wouldn't like me as your CEO."

**Jim Handy:** Yeah.

**Severin Sorensen:** There are things like, you could spot what needs to be done, but the doing and execution, that's another skillset.

**Jim Handy:** Yes. You bring up a really good point and that is really true of me. But I was lucky because I started out with Harry Dennis.

The first time I really had a business, it was a partnership, and we were the opposite. One time I was in the bathroom and two people were on the other side talking that we had just met with us and they said, "Can you believe those two? Can you believe they're in the same company together? Handy's this way and Dennis..." But everything I didn't like and wasn't good at, Harry was good at and vice versa.

I'm really glad you brought that up because that was huge. And so, I would go out and expand and Harry would make sure, "Okay, the I's are dotted, the T's are crossed. We're making money on this thing. The things are flowing in. We're doing this, we're doing that." As a partner I had to fly my craziness by him and vice versa. I couldn't get too crazy because I had to bring him along. And vice versa with him. He would say, "Okay, we've gotta do this now." "Geez, Harry, that sounds slogging." And he explained it. "Okay. You're right."

It was perfect. And so, when I started the Paranet Group, the first thing I did is I looked to hire someone who I looked at as a partner. They liked the stuff I didn't like. I couldn't run operations. Shoot me now! I'd be great the first time I did something. Not too bad the second.

You don't want me doing it the fifth time!

I didn't mean to get off on that, but you asked me about the past. That is probably one of the biggest things. I was just lucky that I fell into it in the beginning and Harry and I had absolute trust in each other. So, it was split 50/50. He said, "I don't want to get on a plane." So, I was in Philadelphia and Cleveland and Minneapolis and so forth.

**Severin Sorensen:** I think having a complimentary partner there that can balance you like the yin and yang, so you have the whole is so important. I certainly find in hiring talent, if you could hire two people at the same time in a similar role, they help and support each other in ways where one person might be quite lonely and not know how to go through that journey. So that's interesting.

**Jim Handy:** And then learn to build a trust between them.

**Severin Sorensen:** Yeah.

**Jim Handy:** They don't see themselves as competitors.

**Severin Sorensen:** Was there a tough or a difficult moment in your business journey and how did you overcome that?

**Jim Handy:** Probably the closest was early on when I was laying in that bed in Green Bay and saying, "Is this really what I want to do?"

And as we've just talked, I'm not one that does the same thing forever. I think the decision was, "Am I ready to move on or am I ready to start to have an impact on TEC? And am I ready to have an impact on TEC that fits what I do and am I any good at doing that?"

That was probably the toughest decision. And I said, "I can't spend my life running around from one thing to another here. I'm now 35." And so, that was probably the toughest one, but it worked out.

**Severin Sorensen:** Oh, that's great. If you were to write a book, maybe you've already written one on the biography of your life, the autobiography, what would the title be for your book?

**Jim Handy:** *"I Didn't Really Think I'd Be Very Good."*

**Severin Sorensen:** Is that the title? *"I Didn't Think I'd Be Very Good!"* Yeah. I could see thousands of people wanting that book.

**Jim Handy:** Yeah. I grew up in a working-class family. I really did have ADHD when no one knew what it was, going to school in the forties. So, it wasn't a real confidence builder. For a long time, I thought, "Geez, I'm just skimming by and nobody really knows that I don't know what the hell I'm doing."

Somewhere along the line I learned that, "Wait a second, you seem to know what you're doing!" Frankly, at some level it would probably be that transition more than things that I did. I was in the Army as I said, and that was probably the best thing I did. That was... the next generation, or a few years later, people took a gap year. We didn't take a gap year. When you couldn't figure out what you're doing, you joined the Army. It was a peacetime army as pre-Vietnam, and that matured me. And coming out of that is when I started to get a grip and started to say, "Wait a second! One, you're smart. You never thought you were smart, but it turns out you're smart." and I finished college and went on to other things. So, it would really be, that'd probably be the title. *I Didn't Think I'd Be Any Good.* I don't know if I want to publish that, but I never thought of that before.

**Severin Sorensen:** Words have wings. I will not make that the title of this episode. I would like people to listen to the episode.

**Jim Handy:** Yeah, so I'm always... yeah, needing whatever you want to call a problem, a quest, a new, silver, shiny thing to follow. Does that make any sense?

**Severin Sorensen:** It's your answer, so it makes great sense.

**Jim Handy:** I would rather go as a team than alone.

**Severin Sorensen:** Go with others. Yeah.

**Jim Handy:** Maybe, probably lead them, but go with them.

Keepers of the Flame 2021

**Severin Sorensen:** So maybe the name of the book would be *Don't Go It Alone.*

**Jim Handy:** Yeah! *Don't Go It Alone.*

**Severin Sorensen:** All right. Getting close to the end here. I love to ask this question. I was moved several years ago by a book that Clayton Christensen wrote prior to his passing called, *"How Will You Measure Your Life?"* How will you measure your life?

**Jim Handy:** I don't consider myself all that good at it, but it's going to have something to do with relationships; of the impact that I've had. When I think back at the highlights, they're almost never the business. It's the impact I might have had on people, careers, and things like that. One guy wrote a book, and he acknowledged me in the forward and things like that mean more to me than probably anything. So, I just... yeah... cared.

**Severin Sorensen:** Okay. Thank you. What is the question I've not asked you that would tell us more about you?

**Jim Handy:** Boy you've covered the waterfront. I think I've... I can't think of it. I talk about that I like all kinds of new things and people and leadership and business and models and I just, I can't think, I'm sorry. I can't think of anything.

**Severin Sorensen:** It's all good. And again, that's your answer. That's fine. Yeah, go ahead.

**Jim Handy:** Can I ask you a question? What was your business? What did you do?

**Severin Sorensen:** I've had close to 20 different businesses. When I was a Vistage member, I had a company that was a low voltage electrical company doing installation of access control, CCTV, intercom speaker-type systems. We also did threat assessments. We did monitored systems. And then the thing that we did that blew up in a very good way was we were in the early days of remote video monitoring. We built out systems, but also automated ways of doing monitoring. And so that was something that was fun to.

**Jim Handy:** Ah, okay. Ah, interesting. That's really, that world has really exploded.

**Severin Sorensen:** Oh, it has, yeah. Many things that were just demos at that time are quite advanced in use right now. So, it was a technology business, but I also learned several things about business models along the way...that when you choose a technology thread, make sure you have the budget and time for that.

I can recall a business that I invested in with a partner, that after about $350,000 in expense and 9 generations of software and about 5 hardware platform changes, we were like, "You know what? We don't have the budget to play like the big boys. We have the ideas and the keenness, but we can't play like the big guys on this. This is not something that we're going to lead in, even though what we have is pretty cool."

Sometimes ideas are too big. It reminds me like, years ago, I was fascinated at the beginning of the internet, and I started a web page development company, and I started with three partners and we started, and then I dissolved the partnership in the first month because I was getting all the sales, I was doing all the coding, I was doing all the work, and I don't know what my drone-bee partners were doing, but they were not participating. And I'm like, "All right, this partnership is not working." They thought the partnership was working great, by the way, and I'm like, "This is not working for me." I said, "But my other concern is the market is too big and a concern I have is that Microsoft or some other company is going to come in and do it." And sure enough, six months later, a Front Page came out, which was the application software to help people do it.

**Jim Handy:** Yeah.

**Severin Sorensen:** And to commoditize it. And in many respects, I see the same thing today with AI. I love what I'm seeing with AI. I think there's tons of opportunity, but to go in there and do a niche is the only way to survive right now. Because the large players are just slugging it out and it's going to be like Clayton Christensen's innovator's dilemma all over again. 125 companies going to be the hard drive manufacturer and 5 survived.

**Jim Handy:** Yeah.

**Severin Sorensen:** And I see there's going to be a ton of people lose money in their quest to make amazing projects.

**Jim Handy:** Yeah.

**Severin Sorensen:** In fact, I think I have to say... I like OpenAI and ChatGPT, but I'm really waiting for the better version of Google Bard to come out because of some of the components that are there. And I think Sam Altman and OpenAI are so smart to sell out now everything they have before those others get there. It will be viewed as being the execution model for "Get in early, price as such," because when the expansion grows, it's going to be really hard for others to do it.

If you look at the intellectual property around what is going on, there's so much better stuff just behind a kitchen screen that's about to come out. I think it's going to be amazing.

I think knowing a business is another thing I would say you've learned. Knowing when to say when. One of my favorite episodes that, I do interviews like we're doing here where I interview a person from the industry, and we go into their background, but I also do these special topics. So, like the Vistage 65 years was one of the special topics that I really enjoyed. I did an episode on the theme in the Kenny Rogers song, *You Gotta Know When to Hold Em' and When to Fold Em'.*

**Jim Handy:** Yeah.

**Severin Sorensen:** And the whole episode was on how do you as a business owner make that determination? So, for example, you made a determination, "It's time for me to leave TEC and to sell out." And there are things that occur in terms of that. In hindsight, you could say, "Oh, if I'd have kept my Ford Shares, it'd be worth a lot." Yeah, but at the time you don't know that.

**Jim Handy:** Yeah.

**Severin Sorensen:** And at the time, you used your best decision to do that. I think that's one of the things that's so interesting is in the industries I've been in, some of them got so hot. Like I was going out, say the remote video market. I was going out to raise $30 million dollars. And while we were raising the money, we had five offers to take us out completely. And I'm like, "No, I wanna lead in this business." And then it came to me, very directly. "Listen, Severin, we have millions of dollars that you don't have. And if you don't sell to us, we will roll on you and you'll be left like a lone man out there with the scrap of your business because we intend to impoverish all competitors. We are gonna own this." And I'm like, "You know what? If I had pride, I would say 'You're wrong.' But if I were wise, I would say, 'You know what? I think we need to sell it.'"

So, I told my financial advisor at the time, "Alright, we're pivoting right now. We're pivoting. We're going to sell this company, but let's get an auction for it."

And we did.

And it worked out masterfully and good. But what's interesting is my colleagues at the time that were, you know how you have co-opetition? In other words, you have competitors that you are competing with, but you're friends because you're all growing an industry.

**Jim Handy:** Yes.

**Severin Sorensen:** I was the only one of 6 of my peers who sold. And I was the only one that didn't go bankrupt, because the key is that you had to know where and have a sense of how the market is growing and getting too big. Because all these really major competitors came in and then they started giving away the work at lower than cost. So, imagine that you're bidding a job that's a hundred cents and they would bid it at 87 cents on that dollar. And we'll take as much as we can because the recurring revenue had the value, that was the long play. Yeah. But any small entrepreneur would go broke because they could not keep up subsidizing customers as the larger ones. So that was a good exit for me.

That would be one of the lessons: you gotta know when to say when, and you need to know how to take your entry. So, I'm very excited by AI. I love it. I am integrating it. We're doing things, but I am seeking deep niches where these are not the most important niches that large companies are doing, such that I can create a lock on certain threads of the business that I think will have value. And then later on, I think I do perceive another good exit, which will be fun.

**Jim Handy:** Yeah. So, you mean to a different market or to smaller businesses or to...?

**Severin Sorensen:** No, so when I say a niche, you could solve the big problem, but everybody wants to solve the big problem. But if you can figure out how to use a technology in such a way to give economies of scale, to create disruption in an industry, in a pocket of the industry that's large enough to make a difference, but small enough that it doesn't get the first attention of the large capital, I think you can survive. But if you go out right now, like for example, if somebody were to go out right now and say, "I'm gonna change the world of coaching! I'm gonna do this. I think it's a great idea," there's so much money focused on that right now. I think a better thing is to say, "How could I do this and make it reproducible and get the economies of scale?" and then over time, as all the early fruit is taken off the ground, others are going to say, "Now what are the harder problems that can be solved?" And I really go back to, if you're going to innovate, don't choose the easy problem, because there'll be so many competitors soon. Choose the hard problem, execute it, lean it out, figure out how to automate it, and then, as you described, get other people to do that work for you.

**Jim Handy:** Yeah.

**Severin Sorensen:** So that's fun.

**Jim Handy:** Yeah, I got it. Yeah, that's interesting. I have a friend who mentors tech people with apps and concepts and so forth, and like I said, I don't know anything about it, but I hear what you were saying a fair amount where he said, "They don't understand. You've gotta show up with about $350,000 to even start thinking about it." And they, you just can't. It's so hard. You go back to the model of, again, the model of TEC Vistage, my gosh. Three groups would be profitable for Harry, Dennis and I,

**Severin Sorensen:** Oh yeah.

**Jim Handy:** 300 groups or 350 groups. It's just this, it can expand back and forth and it's kind of... yeah. Anyway, it's old school. It's local. As big as it is, someone could go down to Rochester, Minnesota and start it down there because nobody's there, it's a local business.

It's amazing. But I really admire, if I had the smarts and I don't, but the world that you're in, that AI and where that's going. Oh my gosh! What that's going to be doing is just fascinating. I love your idea. Find your little niche, you get over here. No, nobody's looking at you. Yeah.

**Severin Sorensen:** Just go deep. Just go deep. Mine. Literally the word mine, think of just hitting, find that vein of gold and mine. Don't wander off. Go deep, go quickly. Go deliberately into that one pocket that you have, and you'll create something. And later on, people are making a buy, build, or lease decision, and they're like, can we compete against you? What would it cost? If your lead is so far ahead, they have no other alternative than to buy you.

**Jim Handy:** Yeah.

**Severin Sorensen:** If they think they can steal your employees away or they can create it in some other way, then they'll do that.

**Jim Handy:** Yeah. And do I understand you to say you are actively doing this, that this is something you're pursuing?

**Severin Sorensen:** Oh, I am actively creative. I'll put it that way.

**Jim Handy:** Oh, that's fun. That's fun.

**Severin Sorensen:** Oh yeah. There's a lot. People say to me, "How do you have so much time?" I'm like, "Because I'm like you. Once I figure out what needs to be done, I get other people to do it."

**Jim Handy:** Yeah, exactly.

**Severin Sorensen:** Somebody said, "I can't keep up with you." I go, "What do you mean keep up?" "Ah, you're publishing and doing..." I go, "Oh yeah, I got people working on that."

So, it may go out with my name, but I've got quite a cadre of people who are working in addition to also using AI and other tools now as well to kind of make it fun.

**Jim Handy:** Do you find that the trick? I always found the trick was I had to have the person that could reach far enough into my craziness, and I could reach far enough into their day-to-day routine that we could connect sometimes.

**Severin Sorensen:** Oh yeah.

**Jim Handy:** I couldn't, sometimes I couldn't, we couldn't close it either because I was too crazy, or they were too down in the weeds.

**Severin Sorensen:** I appreciate people and I think that's one of my talents, is the ability to appreciate what people can do and figure out how I can leverage their talents to work with me. They don't have to be like me. And we do have to understand each other and so we do a lot of communicating in terms of understanding. But over time, I think the individuals I work with, they get to understand and anticipate what the standard is. And of course, the standard for me is, 'Only your best work will do.' Do your best work at all times, that's enough. I teach people what great work looks like. But when you get it, then it's almost effortless because they understand, they have jobs they really enjoy, and so it's fun, but it's not for everyone. But I'm not... I don't try to hire everyone either.

**Jim Handy:** No, but that's exactly the point. To me that's the fondest memories are finding people were, as I mentioned earlier, TEC was their solution to what they were really good at it. And it fit after a career that just wasn't fitting. Sometimes it was just a matter of a guy from the University of Wisconsin just wasn't making tenure and was getting beat up and that sort of thing.

**Severin Sorensen:** At the end of each of my podcasts, I'd like to summarize what I heard. Can I share with you a few things I heard in our interview today I want to remember?

**Jim Handy:** Yeah, I'm a little nervous, but go ahead.

**Severin Sorensen:** I'll be kind. Okay. So, as I go over this, it was so interesting to me that your early education was in economics with a minor in psychology and that you were quite interested in business and that you took a keen interest in the human potential movement early.

And that particular area brought you in very close alignment to others that were in that area, such as Bob Nourse. You were in the military. You used that experience to help you with the G.I. Bill to get graduate education. Something I highly recommend to others, do what you can to improve yourself, use all the resources that are out there.

You talked that, at one point, is this correct, you were a research resource specialist initially for Bob Nourse and then later you came in ...

**Jim Handy:** When Bob sent letters out, my mentor, who was the resource, referred me to Bob.

**Severin Sorensen:** Okay. Oh, that's excellent. And so, we walked through some of that early work. We had a discussion about the human potential movement. Individuals there that you recall had an impact. Arnold Mendel and Carl Rogers, others that were there. We talked about your early work and your coming in the "presidenting" type role in 1973, is that right? So, when you came in and replaced Frank Sterner, and then we talked about the impact that Purdue Management School had on early TEC and how many of the leaders were there. It was interesting for me to hear that at that time, and it really was a practice as you described, as opposed to a business rolling out; that at the early time of the practice, that the early years, if you were the president, you were also being a Chair, running your own groups at that time. You took over, you had TEC 6, TEC 5, and then as there were other groups that came up. You had shared some of the background work with Fred Cheney, Bill Hall, and others, Harry Dennis all of them had some experience in the area and just how the early days started to grow as TEC Vistage grew over time.

And so, it was interesting. I love the conversation in terms of the, I got into this point of, do you have to be a Renaissance person to do the group? Do you have to be able to do it all? And you talked about at the beginning that you were focused on people who could do the good work, if you will, and that you helped them with leads or other things, but then they had to be able to over time do things.

I think that's a real key issue, is that it's difficult to find people who can do it all. If you can give them the support, you can find people that over time can keep a group full. They might not be able to start a group, but they could keep one full. And I thought that was helpful as well.

I loved your suggestion: good chairs always have a waiting list. I know that I did. And I would give people away that I knew just didn't have a culture that I would envision working with our group. And I would give those away. But others I would say, "Look, we've got a conflict right now with you, with another member because your business' area, but I'd like to put you on a waiting list. We'll either create a new group or there will come a time where one person will sunset out, we'll bring another one in and so on." So that's interesting.

I loved your learnings and lessons from Bob Nourse. In terms of, you described, he did TEC, and he *was* TEC, and how instrumental and formative his early work was and the things that were going on there. And that you liked how you learned from him how to open up the CEO edges, the blind spots as you said, and that Bob was a master of taking a group inside and really getting them to open up. And then the parts that you found wisdom in is to trust the dynamics of the group. The focus on group dynamics, get the group to work together, don't be the answer-person. Get them talking, get them communicating, work with silence, and really go deep when you had that opportunity. I thought that was great.

We talked about your exit, when it came time, and the work you've done since, to volunteering from SCORE. I think all that's really helpful and I just enjoyed the conversation, going back, and learning things about the people you worked with, how you did it. Where I think I really enjoyed the conversation was going back to your earliest days when you were a paper route owner. Okay? And how old were you at that time when you had your first paper route? Do you recall?

**Jim Handy:** I'm thinking 12.

**Severin Sorensen:** Probably at 12. Okay.

**Jim Handy:** Something like that. Yeah.

**Severin Sorensen:** 12-year-old. All right. But what I thought was great is once you figured out the paper route, you got all the other boys to go do the work for you and collect and you can get a candy bar if you go collect all the money and do this other stuff and your quote, *"if it's worth doing, it's worth hiring somebody to get it done."*

Alright, that'll be the new name for this episode title. I can assure you. That's the one that I will remember from today. Yeah, that was great. And it was fun to talk about group work, how you keep volunteers together, and just the overall lessons there. So just thank you.

I think that you've had your fingerprints, your touch, in terms of the growth of TEC-Vistage and how it's gone is remarkable. And just like you have your journey, there are others who will pick that ball up and carry it to the next level. And we each kind of learn what it is that we do so well. Thank you so much for the opportunity to be here today. Thank you.

**Jim Handy:** Thank you. I enjoyed it. Thank you.

**Severin Sorensen:** It's been a lot of fun.

**Severin Sorensen:** So, my guest today is Jim Handy. He is an executive coach, mentor, business advisor, trainer, and former President of TEC Wisconsin.

If you'd like to reach out to Jim, you can reach him in three ways. You can go to his LinkedIn and that is Jim handy. You can go to his email and that is jimlewishandy@gmail.com. Or an easier way perhaps, is to go to MBMentors.org that's mike bravo mentors.org.

With each session of the podcast, I end with a few quotes for you to ponder, and our quotes today come first from Jim Handy, *"If it's worth doing, it's worth hiring somebody to get it done."* Always use leverage. I think that's a great one.

From Sean Hitchcock, *"A mentor empowers a person to see a possible future and believe it can't be obtained."*

Or in the words of Oprah Winfrey, *"A mentor is someone who allows you to see the hope inside yourself."*

And moving on to lifetime learning from Ben Franklin, *"An investment in knowledge pays the best interest."*

Or said even more succinctly by Dr. Seuss, *"The more that you read, the more things you'll know, and the more that you learn, the more places you'll go."*

From Socrates, *"The only true wisdom is knowing you know nothing."* This is certainly something that's been brought to me with AI. The more that I learn, and I have learned quite a bit, the more I know that I absolutely know nothing compared to what's out there.

To summarize these thoughts, the more you learn, the more you grow. The more you grow, the more you know. The more you know, the more you know nothing. And that's a beautiful thing because that's the beginning of wisdom.

Until next time, be your best self, seek to uplift others, be good, and do good. You have been listening to Severin Sorensen and the Arete Coach Podcast, where we explore excellence and the art and science of executive coaching today.

# Appendix
# TEC-Vistage Chairs on the Arete Coach Podcast

These podcasts can be found at AreteCoach.io and on your favorite Podcast App (such as Apple Podcasts, Google Podcasts, Amazon Podcasts, Stitcher, etc.). All these episodes feature individuals that are either current or former TEC-Vistage Chairs (from 2020 through June 2023). Watch or listen to the AreteCoach Podcast at AreteCoach.io or on your favorite podcast app to hear more episodes from TEC-Vistage Chairs.

| Guest Name | Episode | Arete Coach Podcast Title |
| --- | --- | --- |
| Richard Bosworth | 1001 | "Asking What If?" |
| Ozzie Gontang | 1002 | "Asking with listening and skill" |
| Bill Clark | 1004 | "Perseverance in Life" |
| Norma Rosenberg | 1005 | "Intuitive based coaching" |
| Glenn Waring | 1006 | "Challenging, changing, and growing" |
| Steve Ramerini | 1007 | "Prosperity & charity as motivation" |
| Adam Harris | 1008 | "Embracing the Uncomfortable" |
| Larry Cassidy | 1009 | "From Commanding to Coaching" |
| Mikki Williams | 1010 | "Executive presence" |
| Barry Goldberg | 1011 | "Embracing the science of coaching" |
| Jay W Curry | 1013 | "Turning Challenges Into Character" |
| Tim Fulton | 1014 | "Coaching Small Businesses" |
| Katherine Crewe | 1015 | "Adversity, Logic, and Learning" |
| Bud Carter | 1016 | "More Pithy Quotes" |
| Jim Lindell | 1017 | "Controller as Business Manager" |
| Severin Sorensen | 1018 | "Managing Family-Owned Business Leadership Transitions" |
| Phil Holberton | 1019 | "Five Minute Journal" |
| Severin Sorensen | 1021 | "Exploring Powerful Questions" |
| Mark Taylor | 1022 | "Curiosity and Lifetime Learning" |
| Steve Brody | 1025 | "Unanswered Questions Linger Longer" |
| Severin Sorensen | 1026 | "Return to Work" |
| Alan Weinstein | 1029 | "Coaching Entrepreneurship and Management" |
| Jeannette Hobson | 1030 | "Harvesting Accidental Opportunity" |

| | | |
|---|---|---|
| Carol Steinberg | 1031 | "Presume Innocence" |
| Jim Canfield | 1032 | "CEO Tools" |
| Don (Donald) Myers | 1034 | "Power of Referrals"" |
| Janet Fogarty | 1036 | "WAIT = Why Am I Talking" |
| Conor Neill | 1037 | "Powerful Stories Stimulate Action" |
| Allen Hauge | 1038 | "The Economy is The Water We Swim In" |
| Ron Merryman | 1039 | "From Clarity of Vision to Vision With Clarity" |
| Garth Jackson | 1040 | "From Home Builder to Business Builder" |
| Tom Cuthbert | 1041 | "It's Not About Me" |
| Severin Sorensen | 1042 | "Learning From Failure" |
| Severin Sorensen | 1045 | :Golf and Business" |
| Severin Sorensen | 1046 | "Revisiting Powerful Questioning" |
| Severin Sorensen | 1048 | "Knowing Your Kenny Rogers Line" |
| Severin Sorensen | 1050 | "The Great Resignation" |
| Cindy Hesterman | 1051 | "The Seven Solutions Tool" |
| Severin Sorensen | 1052 | "Navigating Inflation" |
| Gail Schaper-Gordon | 1053 | "Being Sentient" |
| Severin Sorensen | 1055 | "Hiring Talent in an Age of Talent Scarcity" |
| Kevin McKeown | 1057 | "On Being A Ripple Maker" |
| Cathy Fitzhenry | 1058 | "Learning from Life's Curriculum" |
| Paul Martin | 1059 | "Dig Deeper" |
| Severin Sorensen | 1063 | "Ukraine Russia Conflict - Freedom Is Not Free" |
| Kevin Rafferty | 1064 | "Coaching Conscious Leaders" |
| Peter Buchanan | 1067 | "Conversation with Co-Founder of TEC-Canada" |
| Severin Sorensen | 1069 | "Economic Outlook Q2 2022" |
| Jason Thompson | 1071 | "On Mastering Balance, Meaning, and Tomatoes"" |
| Severin Sorensen | 1074 | "Navigating Labor Shortage and Wage Inflation" |
| Ken Stibler | 1075 | "From Basketball to Business Coaching and Life's Lessons Learned |

| | | |
|---|---|---|
| Douglas Bouey | 1079 | "On Fixing Fractures and Restoring Shattered Relationships" |
| Tony Lewis | 1080 | "Courage To Fail, Learn, and Think" |
| Severin Sorensen | 1083 | "Surviving Economic Tsunamis" |
| Julie Gammack | 1088 | "Personal Courage, Free Press, and Empowering Writers" |
| Norma Rosenburg | 1089 | "Oops and Ops" and other sage insights |
| Severin Sorensen | 1090 | Honoring Professor Anthony Grant: Father of Evidence Based Coaching |
| Ben Griffin | 1091 | "Exploring CEOIQ and The Leadership Lens" |
| Chip Webster | 1092 | "Act Now and other coach musings" |
| Mike Denning | 1093 | "Serving and Surfing: Lessons in Leadership and Coaching" |
| Michele Barry | 1094 | "Playing on Your Front Foot and Being Offense Minded" |
| Severin Sorensen | 1095 | "10 Things To Take Into A Hard Recession" |
| Virginia Knudsen | 1097 | "So What? Now What?" |
| Severin Sorensen | 1100 | "Curator and Host of the Arete Coach Podcast" |
| Severin Sorensen | 1102 | "Celebrating the 35 Best Executive Coaching Industry Podcasts of 2022" |
| Jim Naleid | 1103 | "Rethink, Unlearn, and Think Again" |
| Severin Sorensen | 1104 | "ChatGPI AI Rocked My World Today" |
| Philip Liebman | 1105 | "Your Mind Is Your Tool" |
| Severin Sorensen | 1106 | "Science of Gratitude" |
| Larry Cassidy, Ozzie Gontang, Ron Greenwood, Severin Sorensen | 1107 | "Coaches Corner: SuperAgers, Lifetime Learning, and AI" |
| Severin Sorensen | 1109 | "Powerful Questioning Revisited" |
| sev@epraxis.com, bill@clarkleadership.com | 1110 | "Bill Clark: Learning from Life's Curriculum" |
| Severin Sorensen | 1112 | "Vistage: Pioneers of Facilitated Peer Executive Groups, 65 Year Anniversary" |
| Severin Sorensen, Ozzie Gontang, Hayden Browning, Cait Pickens | 1114 | "AI, Automation, and the Innovation Imperative" |

| | | |
|---|---|---|
| Ron Greenwood | 1116 | "Science, Statistics, and Inquiry; Life of Professor Ron Greenwood" |
| Severin Sorensen | 1117 | "Beware the Ides of March and Financial Contagion" |
| Pete Michaels | 1118 | "Anticipate: Advice from Executive Coach, Banker, and M&A Specialist" |
| Bridget Wenman | 1120 | "More Grace Less Grief" |
| Severin Sorensen | 1122 | "The AI Whisperer" |
| Jim Handy | 1123 | "If its worth doing, it's worth hiring somebody to do it" |
| Dale Richards | 1124 | "Knowledge is Power" |
| Severin Sorensen | 1125 | Warren Buffett: 40 Lessons from the Oracle of Omaha |
| Severin Sorensen | 1126 | AI Revolution and Jobs to Be Done |
| Severin Sorensen | 1127 | The AI Whisperer Draws |
| Mark Fackler | 1129 | "Love, Learn, and Serve" |
| Perry Maughmer | 1130 | "Mindful Being, Mindful Chairing" |

ABOUT THE AUTHOR:

**Severin Sorensen**

Severin Sorensen is an executive coach and former TEC-Vistage Member (1999-2004), former Vistage Chair (2010 through 2018), former "Vistage Rookie of the Year Chair," former "Mentor Chair," and current Vistage Speaker on AI, Economics, Innovation, and Identifying and Capturing Difference Making Top Talent.

Severin is the curator and host of AreteCoach.io and its podcast that explores the art and science of executive coaching with some of the industry's best coaches, coaching scholars, and book authors. Severin is the author of several best-selling books including: The AI Whisperer Series *(The AI Whisperer, The AI Whisperer Draws),* and other books such as *Next 10 and The Talent Palette.* As CEO of ePraxis LLC (epraxis.com), Severin leads a premier level retained search firm that provides talent selection, executive coaching, and executive headhunting services. In his executive coaching practice, Severin has provided over 8,000+ paid hours of executive coaching to CEOs, business owners, entrepreneurs, and C-level executives. In terms of formal training in coaching, Severin has earned industry recognized ICF ACSTH, Certified Leadership Circle Profile Coach, Certified Organizational Development Coach, Certified Executive Coach, Certified Positive Intelligence Coach, and Certified Life Coach. Severin earned his M.Phil. in Economics at King's College, Cambridge University.

Made in the USA
Coppell, TX
15 June 2023

18137592R00085